COLLINS
IDENTIFYING
BIRDS
BY COLOUR

COLLINS
IDENTIFYING
BIRDS
BY COLOUR

Moss Taylor and Norman Arlott

Collins

Acknowledgements

Moss Taylor would like to thank Peter Kitchener for his
invaluable help in reading through the text.

Norman Arlott would like to thank the staff of the British
Museum, Tring, especially Mark Adams.

Collins
An imprint of HarperCollins Publishers
77-85 Fulham Palace Road
London W6 8JB

www.collins.co.uk

Published in 2008 by HarperCollins Publis

Reprint 10 9 8 7 6 5 4 3 2 1

Copyright text © Moss Taylor 2008
Copyright illustrations © Norman Arlott 2007
and 2008

The author asserts the moral right to be identified
as the author of this work

A catalogue record for this book is available from
the British Library

ISBN-13 978-0-00-720679-7

Cover design by Emma Jern
Designed by Luke Griffin
Colour reproduction by Colourscan, Singapore
Printed and bound in Hong Kong by Printing Express

Contents

 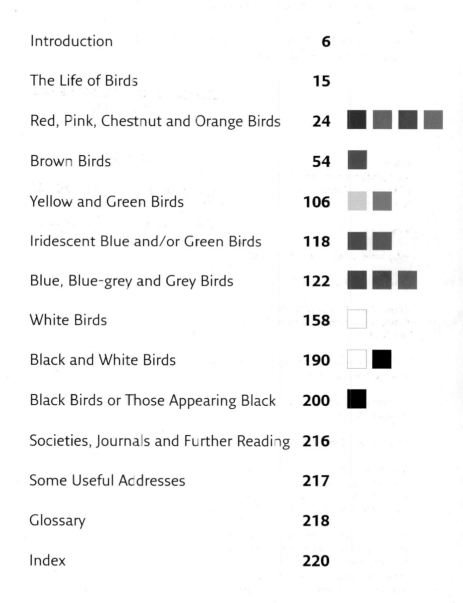

Introduction

Over 50 years ago, a ground-breaking identification book on birds was published
in which the illustrations were arranged by colour – this was the legendary
Collins Pocket Guide to British Birds by Richard Fitter and Richard Richardson.
Since then, the vast majority of identification guides have been based on bird
families, and do not necessarily provide the easiest method for beginners.

Of all the characteristics of birds, colour is the feature that most often
attracts attention, especially among those who do not have a particular interest
in this fascinating field of natural history. In describing an unidentified bird,
a non-birdwatcher inevitably starts with the colour or colours of the mystery
species. But basing a search simply on colour (and even size), it would not
be easy for a beginner to trawl through a standard field guide, arranged in
traditional family order, and arrive at a correct identification. How much easier
then if all the birds were simply arranged according to their dominant or most
distinctive colour(s).

About this book

In this book you will find over 250 species of bird arranged by colour. Many
species appear just once (or twice if the sexes are markedly different in colour)
in the section that contains their main colour. Others, however, such as the
Great Tit, possess a variety of distinctive colours and may therefore appear
several times. In general, birds whose main colour is present in all the body
plumage are shown first, followed by those in which the colour is confined
to the head, underparts or upperparts.

With its all-white plumage,
the Little Egret features only
once, in the white section.

female

male

The Blackbird appears twice –
the male in the black section,
the female in the brown.

With its black cap,
yellow breast and
blue-grey wings, the
Great Tit appears
several times.

Within each colour section the birds are further arranged into three main groups which are themselve subdivided as follows: land birds (including birds of prey, owls and game birds), marsh birds and waders, and waterbirds (including seabirds). Although the order of colours is somewhat arbitrary, they do roughly follow the colours of the rainbow, commencing with the reds (red, pink, chestnut and orange), through brown, yellow, green, blue and grey, to white and finally black. There is also a black and white section that includes birds showing a combination of these two colours, and which are not repeated separately in both the black and the white sections. On the whole, birds are not shown in flight, because colour is rarely used for identifying birds in the air. But where a colour feature is best seen in flight – such as a chestnut rump or white wing bars – birds are also shown flying.

Of course, features other than colour are used in bird identification, some of which have been alluded to above, such as size and the habitat in which a bird is usually found. Other clues might be shape, type of bill, leg length, voice and behaviour, some of which are expanded on below. Any such additional characteristics are also included in the species accounts accompanying the illustrations.

As well as the illustrations and species texts, this book contains an introduction to the daily lives of birds, some tips for novice birdwatchers, a glossary of some of the terms used in the text and suggestions for further reading. It is very much meant as a basic introduction to bird identification for readers of all ages, using colour as the initial means of recognising the commonest species that occur in Britain and Ireland.

Which birds are included?

About 190 species breed annually in Britain and Ireland and many others occur in winter or on migration. One of the problems for beginners is separating out those species they are most likely to record during their early birdwatching days from those they are least likely to see. Not doing so can easily lead to errors in identification. It's always worth remembering that common birds occur commonly and by definition rarities are just that – rare!

This book, then, largely confines itself to those species that are regularly recorded in Britain and Ireland in a genuinely wild state, including all those that breed annually. Only a few rarer species are included. The selection is, to a certain extent, an arbitrary one and readers may well feel that other species should have been included, while some should have been omitted. In addition, some birds, such as the Rose-ringed Parakeet, have been featured because they are seen regularly as escapes or feral birds and rarely pass unnoticed! In general, subspecies (races) are not included unless they occur relatively frequently and are readily identifiable in the field.

For most species, the illustrations are confined to adults, with both sexes illustrated only where there are noticeable plumage differences between the two. With the exception of swans, immature birds are not included. Where there is a marked difference between the breeding and non-breeding plumages of a bird, such as the Golden Plover, both may be illustrated in the relevant colour sections.

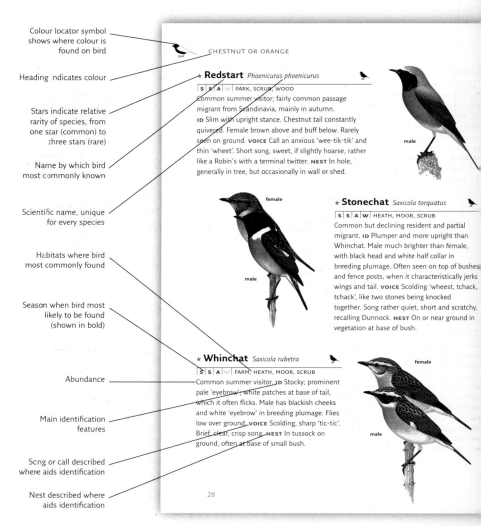

Colour locator symbol shows where colour is found on bird

Heading indicates colour

Stars indicate relative rarity of species, from one star (common) to three stars (rare)

Name by which bird most commonly known

Scientific name, unique for every species

Habitats where bird most commonly found

Season when bird most likely to be found (shown in bold)

Abundance

Main identification features

Song or call described where aids identification

Nest described where aids identification

CHESTNUT OR ORANGE

★ **Redstart** *Phoenicurus phoenicurus*
S S A W PARK, SCRUB, WOOD
Common summer visitor; fairly common passage migrant from Scandinavia, mainly in autumn.
ID Slim with upright stance. Chestnut tail constantly quivered. Female brown above and buff below. Rarely seen on ground. **VOICE** Call an anxious 'wee-tik-tik' and thin 'wheet'. Short song, sweet, if slightly hoarse, rather like a Robin's with a terminal twitter. **NEST** In hole, generally in tree, but occasionally in wall or shed.

male

female

★ **Stonechat** *Saxicola torquatus*
S S A W HEATH, MOOR, SCRUB
Common but declining resident and partial migrant. **ID** Plumper and more upright than Whinchat. Male much brighter than female, with black head and white half collar in breeding plumage. Often seen on top of bushes and fence posts, when it characteristically jerks wings and tail. **VOICE** Scolding 'wheest, tchack, tchack', like two stones being knocked together. Song rather quiet, short and scratchy, recalling Dunnock. **NEST** On or near ground in vegetation at base of bush.

male

★ **Whinchat** *Saxicola rubetra*
S S A W FARM, HEATH, MOOR, SCRUB
Common summer visitor. **ID** Stocky; prominent pale 'eyebrow'; white patches at base of tail, which it often flicks. Male has blackish cheeks and white 'eyebrow' in breeding plumage. Flies low over ground. **VOICE** Scolding, sharp 'tic-tic'. Brief, clear, crisp song. **NEST** In tussock on ground, often at base of small bush.

female

male

28

How to use this book

This book has been designed to make the identification of birds as easy as possible for beginners. When looking up a bird, start by going to the appropriate colour section, marked by a coloured bar along the edge of the right-hand page. Then turn to the required bird type (for example, land bird, bird of prey, wader, waterbird) and look through the illustrations until you find the one matching your bird. If the colour is restricted to a specific area, such as the underparts, head or rump, you can also use the colour locator symbols to help you find the bird you are looking for.

SMALL LAND BIRDS

Heading indicates type of bird

★ **Chaffinch** *Fringilla coelebs*

S | S | A | W FARM, GARDEN, HEATH, PARK, WOOD

Abundant resident and winter visitor mainly from Scandinavia. **ID** One of our most widespread birds and the second commonest. Double white wing bars and white sides to tail. Female uniformly buff. In winter sexes often found in separate flocks. **VOICE** Cheerful 'spink' and a difficult to locate 'hooeet'. Song a vigorous cascade with a terminal flourish, tirelessly repeated after a short interval and often followed by a nearby rival's song. **NEST** In fork of tree or bush.

male

Colour bar indicates colour(s) featured on both pages

Gender given where sexes differ (also breeding and non-breeding)

★★ **Hawfinch**
Coccothraustes coccothraustes   >

S | S | A | W PARK, WOOD

Fairly common but localised resident. **ID** A large finch with a very powerful, heavy bill. Strange club-shaped extensions on inner primaries. In flight prominent white tip to tail and white wing bar. Often found in vicinity of Hornbeams. Very wary and despite flocking in winter can be extremely elusive. **VOICE** A Robin-like 'tzic'. **NEST** On horizontal branch of tree at varying height, often in loose colony of a few pairs.

Size comparison (see key overleaf for details). > means larger than, < means smaller than

★★ **Kingfisher** *Alcedo atthis*   >

S | S | A | W FRESH

Fairly common resident. **ID** One of our most colourful birds, but often smaller than imagined; rather dumpy and short tailed with a long, dagger-shaped bill. Sexes similar but male has all-black bill throughout year. Perches upright, but despite bright colours can be remarkably well camouflaged when sitting in shadow; plunges into water to catch small fish, occasionally hovering before diving; flies like an arrow low over water. **VOICE** A piping, metallic 'tzi' in flight. **NEST** In tunnelled hole in sandy bank.

Illustration shows bird with featured colour. Where male and female plumage differs, look in appropriate sections of book

25

9

Relative rarity value

While it can be exciting to see any species, particularly when first taking up birdwatching, it is always more satisfying to find and identify the less common birds. With this in mind, and in an attempt to classify their relative scarcity value, species are rated in increasing rarity as one-, two- or three-star birds. It must be remembered, however, that what is common in the south of England may be rare in Scotland or Ireland, and vice versa. Thus the Jay is given one star and yet is virtually unknown in the far north of Scotland, while the White-tailed Eagle is given three stars but may well be seen almost daily by residents of some of the Scottish isles. Some of the least common birds are ones that occur in Britain and Ireland only as migrants, usually in the spring or autumn.

The naming of birds

Unfortunately, English bird names have been going through a period of change in recent years and it is almost impossible to arrive at a standard list that is acceptable to all organisations and journals. The names used in this book are those that are most often used by birdwatchers in Britain and Ireland. To overcome this problem, and to be absolutely clear which species is being described, the scientific name is also given after the more familiar English one. The binomial system that uses two Latin words is universally recognised and is unique for every species, although even these names have been updated recently in the light of new DNA research.

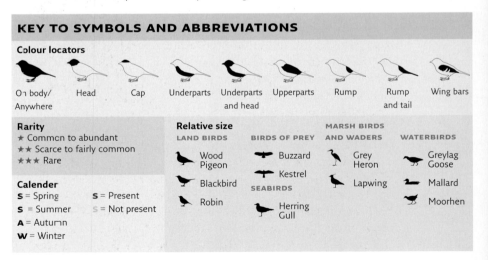

KEY TO SYMBOLS AND ABBREVIATIONS

Colour locators

On body/Anywhere · Head · Cap · Underparts · Underparts and head · Upperparts · Rump · Rump and tail · Wing bars

Rarity
★ Common to abundant
★★ Scarce to fairly common
★★★ Rare

Calender
S = Spring
S = Summer
A = Autumn
W = Winter

s = Present
s = Not present

Relative size

LAND BIRDS
Wood Pigeon
Blackbird
Robin

BIRDS OF PREY
Buzzard
Kestrel

SEABIRDS
Herring Gull

MARSH BIRDS AND WADERS
Grey Heron
Lapwing

WATERBIRDS
Greylag Goose
Mallard
Moorhen

Relative sizes of birds

Most books on bird identification give absolute measurements of the birds' length and wingspan in centimetres. These figures actually mean very little to most people. The system adopted in this book is to compare the size of each bird with the silhouettes of up to three common species that occupy the same habitat and are likely to be recognised by most readers. Thus land birds are compared with a Wood Pigeon, Blackbird or Robin, marsh birds and waders with a Heron or Lapwing, waterbirds with a Greylag Goose, Mallard or Moorhen, and seabirds with a Herring Gull. The only exceptions are the birds of prey, which are compared with a Buzzard or Kestrel. Size comparisons are only approximations and take into account the general appearance of the bird in the field. Where the size is noticeably larger (>) or smaller (<) than the comparative species, this is denoted by the appropriate symbol. Note that colour illustrations on a page are not shown in relative size to each other.

At which time of year are birds likely to be seen?

While many species, such as House Sparrows and Pheasants, are resident in Britain and Ireland, others are normally present only at certain times of the year – for example, Swallows in the summer and Fieldfares in the winter.

Other species occur only as they pass through on spring and autumn migration, but these tend to be the rarer birds and so only a few of them, such as the Hoopoe and Bluethroat, are included in this book. To provide readers with a rough guide as to when a species is most likely to be seen, the year has been divided into the four seasons defined as follows: spring (March–May), summer (June–August), autumn (September–November) and winter (December–February).

The Hoopoe is a rare passage migrant, only seen in spring and autumn.

Where are birds most likely to be seen?

As with the seasons, there are no hard and fast rules, and many birds could turn up in almost any habitat, especially while on migration. However, the usual habitats in which the species are most likely to be found include: buildings, coast, farm, freshwater (fresh), garden, heath, marsh, moorland (moor), mountain, parkland (park), reedbed (reeds), scrub and woodland (wood). For each species the habitats are shown alphabetically and do not denote any order of preference or likelihood. Thus by referring to the habitats it is possible to see that a small brown bird in a wood is far more likely to be a Garden Warbler than a Reed Warbler.

How abundant is each species?

The species texts commence with a short statement giving the bird's abundance and status within Britain and Ireland. The general breeding area of winter visitors, passage migrants and vagrants is also given (for an explanation of these terms, see the glossary). The categories of abundance are defined as follows:

	Pairs in summer	Count at other seasons
Rare	1 – 100	1 – 200
Scarce	101 – 1000	201 – 2000
Fairly common	1001 – 10,000	2001 – 20,000
Common	10,001 – 100,000	20,001 – 200,000
Very common	100,001 – 1,000,000	200,001 – 2,000,000
Abundant	> 1,000,000	> 2,000,000

Main identification features (ID)

This section of the species texts highlights the main identification features, including comparative size, shape and structure, behaviour and, if appropriate, races or colour morphs. In general, plumage details are not included, as these are shown in the illustrations. The main exceptions are where differences occur between the sexes. Juveniles tend to have similar colouring to the females, so, except in a few instances (such as gulls and swans), they are not described or illustrated. The page numbers of any additional illustrations of a species (that is, males or females) can be found by referring to the index.

Voice

The songs or calls of a bird are included only if they can be used as an aid to identification and can be fairly easily learnt by a beginner. Many are given in general terms rather than as phonetic transcriptions. Most passerines (small perching birds) have a song that is used by the male to attract a mate and to define its territory. Simple calls tend to be given in flight to maintain contact with other members of the same species or as warning signals when danger threatens. Most birds use calls, even if they never sing.

Nest

Details of typical nest sites are given only for those species that breed in Britain and Ireland, and have been included if the information is likely to be useful in helping to identify a species – for instance, if it is accidentally disturbed from its nest.

Parts of a bird

Many different terms are used throught this book to describe the various parts of a bird, many of which can be found in the glossary on page 218. The illustration below shows the major features of a bird. In describing a bird it is important to be able to convey accurately the position of any outstanding features. This particularly applies to the head and closed wing, and it is well worth learning the correct anatomical terms and their exact location on a bird.

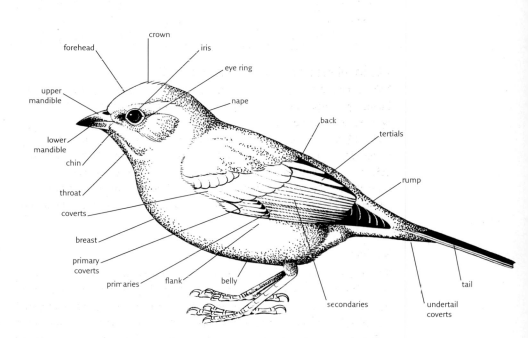

TAKING UP BIRDWATCHING AS A HOBBY

Birdwatching is an increasingly popular pursuit, no doubt aided by the considerable improvement in optical aids and cameras, as well as concern for the environment. Spend as much as time as possible studying birds at first hand, be it in your garden or in the wider countryside, and try to learn the songs and calls of the commoner ones, adding the voices of new species as your birdwatching progresses. Although songs and calls can be learnt from CDs or preferably DVDs, by far the best method is to go out with a more experienced birdwatcher who already knows them.

Binoculars Although it is possible to watch birds, at least those that are reasonably close, without using binoculars, their use enables us to appreciate the finer points of the birds' plumage and to watch their fascinating behaviour from a distance without disturbing them. Choosing the most suitable pair of binoculars is very much a personal matter. Factors to consider are magnification, brightness of image, size, weight and, perhaps most important of all, price. The specification of a pair of binoculars is denoted by two figures, for example 10 x 42. The first figure refers to the magnification and the second to the diameter in millimetres of the objective lens (the lens nearest to the object). Prices vary from under £100 to almost ten times that amount, but for a beginner a pair costing about £150 should be ideal. The golden rule is to try them out before purchase – do not simply buy a pair on the strength of an advert!

Taking notes Next to binoculars, a notebook and pencil are the most important things to take with you in the field. Ink runs in wet weather, so making notes with a pencil is preferable. Descriptive notes made at the time of observation are much more valuable than those written later, as are sketches of the birds, no matter how basic. Numbers of each species seen are also useful, whether for future reference or for reporting sightings to the county bird recorder.

What to wear Finally, wearing the most appropriate clothing is paramount if you wish to obtain maximum enjoyment from your hobby. Neutral colours, such as olive green, are preferable to bright ones, often enabling a much closer approach to the birds without disturbing them. Footwear appropriate to the type of habitats you are likely to cross is also important: sturdy trainers or light walking boots are generally suitable.

The Life of Birds

This identification guide is based on the remarkable variation in the plumage found in birds, which is dependent on the colours of their feathers – the one unique feature that sets birds apart from all other living creatures. The anatomical structure of feathers varies according to their function, some being responsible for insulation, others for display or camouflage, and yet others for flight.

The small, downy feathers nearest to the bird's body act as insulation against the effects of cold and are capable of being fluffed up, thus trapping a layer of warm air; they also aid waterproofing. Overlying these down feathers are the so-called contour feathers, which dictate the colour of a bird's head and body plumage. In general, the more brightly coloured feathers are used in display, either in attracting a mate or in repelling a rival. For this reason, in the majority of species, the males have the brighter plumage, whilst the females are more soberly attired. For example, many female ducks are brown to provide camouflage on the nest. Specialised contour feathers are found in the wings and tail; these tend to be stiffer than the others and are concerned with flight.

The perceived colours in a bird's plumage arise from two sources: pigments contained within the feathers and the microscopic structure of the feather itself. In general, the blacks and browns are melanins (pigments) that are produced by the birds, while carotenoids, taken in with food, are deposited in the feathers (as well as the skin) and are responsible for the yellows, oranges and reds. Structural colours account for the blue, green and purple iridescence seen in, for example, crows, starlings and ducks.

female

male

The male Pheasant has a much brighter plumage than the female.

Feather care

All birds need to spend a significant part of each day on preening and other activities associated with feather care, in order for the feathers to function effectively. Feathers are remarkably strong and long-lasting considering their rather flimsy structure, and part of a bird's preening activity is concerned with ensuring that the constituent parts of each individual feather are 'hooked' together satisfactorily. Waterproofing is achieved by obtaining oil from the preen gland (the 'parson's nose' of a roast chicken) and spreading the oil amongst the plumage by means of its bill. Preening also removes any toxic substances or parasites from the feathers, as does 'anting', an activity in which ants run through a bird's plumage and are believed to release formic acid, which aids the cleaning process. Whatever the exact means, the birds clearly enjoy it and appear to go into a trance during the anting behaviour, as they also do when sunning themselves.

A Whinchat preens its feathers with its beak to keep them in good condition.

A Jay allows ants to run through its plumage as part of its cleaning process.

Moult

Of course, feathers do not last for ever and need to be replaced as they wear out or become damaged. In many species, adults undergo a complete moult of all their feathers annually after the breeding season. The feathers are replaced in sequence, which means that in the vast majority of species the power of flight is retained. One exception to this is wildfowl, which shed all their flight feathers at the same time, so that for a period, while the new wing feathers are growing, the birds are flightless. It is for this reason that the brightly coloured adult drakes undergo an additional moult in late summer, and adopt the colours of the drabber females. This so-called 'eclipse' plumage is retained for the time that the drake is flightless.

Moult places great demands on a bird's reserves and therefore it takes place after the breeding season, either before or after autumn migration. It is a relatively rapid process in those species that moult prior to migration, such as the Blackcap, and is completed in 35 days; however, in a resident species, like the Bullfinch, where speed is less important, it takes up to 85 days.

In most species, moult in juveniles is restricted to the head and body plumage, and to a partial replacement of the wing coverts. The tail and flight feathers are retained until the full moult in the late summer or autumn of the second year, a fact used by ringers when ageing birds in the hand.

At other times of the year, any feathers lost accidentally or through trauma are replaced soon after the loss.

Development of breeding plumage

In late winter or early spring, some species undergo an additional body and head moult that results in the appearance of their breeding plumage. Many waders have white underparts during the winter, moulting to black or red for the summer. For example, Grey and Golden Plovers have extensive black breasts and bellies, while Knots and Bar-tailed Godwits show rich chestnut underparts in summer. Another very obvious change is the chocolate-brown head of a summer-plumaged Black-headed Gull, which appears as a result of a late-winter moult involving the feathers on the head.

However, for the majority of passerines, or small perching birds, it is simply a matter of the feather tips wearing away as winter progresses, to expose the more intense colours further down the shaft. Take, for example, Starlings. During winter, their plumage is characterised by extensive white or pale spotting, especially on the underparts. As the white feather tips wear away, the glossy iridescence of their breeding dress is gradually revealed. The same process is responsible for the appearance in spring of the blue crown of the Chaffinch and the uniformly black head and orange breast of the male Brambling, which makes it such a striking bird at that time of year.

Courtship display

Courtship plays an important role in ensuring that birds recognise others of the same species, find a member of the opposite sex and hopefully pair up and successfully raise young. The brightly coloured feathers of male birds are often part of this courtship display, along with the individual songs that are unique to each species. The greatest diversity of colour is often found amongst groups of birds in which several similar species gather to display in the same general area. This is particularly well shown in the smaller wildfowl.

You have only to look at the plumage patterns and distribution of colours in drakes, compared with the

non-breeding

breeding

The breeding plumage of the Knot is related to both display and camouflage.

17

rather plain, mottled brown of most ducks, to appreciate the great variety that exists. In fact, sorting out unaccompanied female ducks can be one of the most difficult identification problems for birdwatchers. Clearly, the females are attracted to drakes exhibiting specific colours and patterns, often around the head and neck, and shown to their best advantage by the exaggerated head movements used by many species. In other birds, such as the Great Crested Grebe, there is very little sexual dimorphism – that is, difference in the appearance of the two sexes. In this species both birds take an equally active role when performing their highly ritualised displays. The commonest of these is the appropriately named 'head-shaking ceremony', when the pair face each other with their necks erect, shaking their heads slowly from side to side.

In general, in those species that construct open nests, the females are dull brown to avoid detection during incubation, while in hole-nesting birds they are often nearly as brightly coloured as the males, a good example being the Blue Tit. The same even holds true for the Shelduck, which typically nests underground in a rabbit burrow.

But perhaps the most interesting examples of sexual dimorphism occur in the Dotterel and phalaropes, species of wader that demonstrate almost complete role reversal. The more brightly coloured females display to the duller-plumaged males and, once mating has occurred and the clutch has been completed, it is the males' responsibility to incubate the eggs and take care of the young, thus allowing the females to find another mate and make the most of the short northern summer.

Songs and calls

In passerines, attracting a potential mate and establishing a breeding territory is also achieved by the use of songs and calls. As the breeding cycle progresses, males tend to sing less and become more involved in parental duties. Although singing is mainly confined to male birds, females are capable of it – it is just that the tendency to burst into song is latent. However, the females of certain species do sing, including Robins during the winter months. As birds age and hormonal imbalances occur, females tend to start singing, a fact that is well known to breeders of Canaries.

Famed for its voice, the male Nightingale has a loud and musical song.

Nesting

Of all birds' activities, surely one of the most amazing is their ability to construct nests. While many non-passerines make only token nests, such as the shallow scrapes used by waders, other birds build the most complicated structures, many of which would severely test human engineering skills. Undoubtedly birds' eggs are objects of great beauty, the remarkable variety in colour and markings having evolved over countless millennia to aid the survival of the individual species. Those laid in open, cup-shaped nests or simple scrapes on the ground tend to be brown or greenish, with an irregular pattern of darker marks providing camouflage against potential predators, while the eggs of many hole-nesting birds are plain white or very pale in colour, as there is no need for camouflage.

The marvel of migration

While certain insect-eating birds, such as the Long-tailed Tit, Wren, Treecreeper and Goldcrest, are resident in Britain and Ireland, the vast majority, like the Swallow and the warblers, are summer visitors, spending the cold winter months in the warmer climes of southern Europe or Africa. Prior to migration in the autumn, a Whitethroat, for example, will change from its normal diet of insects to fruits and berries, foods rich in carbohydrates that will be converted to fat, which is laid down under the skin and can be utilised as fuel during the bird's long flight to its West African wintering grounds. At the same time, the flight muscles increase in size, again in preparation for migration. During this period, a bird's weight can almost double. Once the optimum weight for migration has been reached, the bird will bide its time until suitable weather conditions occur. On the afternoon of departure, it will rest rather than feed, and under cover of darkness will begin its journey south. In the case of a Whitethroat, this will consist of short flights of about 80km each night. By migrating at night the Whitethroat can avoid the attention of any predators and is able to utilise the daylight hours not only for rest, but also to take on additional food, which will again be converted into fat for the continuation of its journey.

The Swallow is a common summer visitor to our shores.

While Whitethroats migrate singly and at night, many birds, such as Swallows and House Martins, migrate by day and in company with others of the same or similar species. By feeding while on the wing, they tend not to accumulate fat and thus have little or no reserves should they encounter bad weather on their migratory journey. Not all species migrate on a north–south axis, as warblers and Swallows do. Many travel west in autumn from northern and eastern Europe to spend the winter months in the comparatively mild climes of western Europe. For example, many wildfowl and thrushes winter in Britain and Ireland and return to their more northern and eastern breeding areas in spring. Some of them, such as the geese and wild swans, travel in family parties and remain together throughout the winter. Birdwatchers in Britain and Ireland are also ideally placed to witness the enormous variety of passage migrants that simply pass along the coastline on their journeys between their breeding and wintering grounds.

The exact methods by which birds are able to navigate over such great distances have long been a mystery, but careful research is at last beginning to unravel this truly amazing feat. It appears that migrating birds use three main compasses: the sun, the stars and the earth's magnetic field. To these must be added the inborn 'knowledge' as to which direction and for how long a bird needs to fly on its migratory journey each spring and again on its return flight in autumn.

Feeding adaptations

A good clue as to the type of food a bird takes is the shape and size of its bill. The familiar, broad, triangular bills of finches are designed to allow the birds to remove the hard outer case of a nut and reach the kernel inside. This design is taken to the extreme in the Hawfinch, which has a massively heavy bill for the size of the bird, so powerful that it can crack open even cherry stones. At the other extreme, the narrow, pointed bill of a Goldfinch allows it to extract seeds from the heads of teasels, while the bills of Crossbills are specially shaped to allow the birds to extract seeds from fir cones.

The bills of many insectivorous birds, such as the Willow Warbler, are thin and pointed, enabling them to delicately pick up spiders and small non-flying insects. Then there are those species, such as the Spotted Flycatcher, that feed predominantly by waiting on an exposed branch, from where they make forays to catch insects on the wing. In these, the bill is pointed but much broader at the base, thus increasing the potential catching area.

Between these two extremes of a broad, finch-like bill and a fine, insectivorous one is that possessed by the non-specialist feeders. These birds take a wide variety of food items from berries and other fruit to worms and insects such as leatherjackets. Many of our familiar garden birds fall into

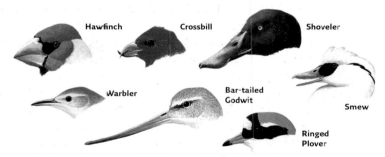

A bird's bill is well adapted to the bird's method of feeding.

this category – Starlings and Blackbirds, for instance. It is also, of course, these omnivorous species that readily take food we put out for them.

There is an even greater variety of bill shapes and sizes in species associated with wetlands. While the majority of surface-feeding ducks all share the same basic design with a rather broad, flat, elongated bill, this is taken to extreme in the Shoveller, as its name suggests. In this species the bill is particularly long and gives the duck a very distinct and somewhat ungainly profile. But it does make an ideal 'shovel' with which to scoop up food from the water surface, as the bird swims around feeding. Diving ducks that catch fish underwater, such as the Goosander and Smew, have narrow bills with teeth-like serrations along the sides that enable them to get a better grip on their slippery prey. For this reason, the group as a whole are known as sawbills.

The strange and well-known shape of the Puffin's bill is also partly an adaptation to its underwater exploits. Puffins often have to fly many kilometres from their nesting burrows to fishing grounds far out to sea. The size and shape of their bills allow them to carry home up to ten small fish or sand eels, arranged head to tail crosswise along the length of the bill.

Among the wading birds, surface-feeders show a great diversity, from the delicate, upturned bill of the Avocet to the very long, flat, spoon-shaped bill of the aptly named Spoonbill. Both of these very different designs allow the birds to sweep the surface of the water, from side to side, filtering out invertebrates and, in the case of the Spoonbill, catching small fish and even frogs. Waders that tend to pick food from or near the surface of the mud, like the Ringed Plover, have short, often rather stout bills, while those that probe more deeply, such as the Bar-tailed Godwit, have long bills that enable them to reach invertebrates that are out of the reach of shorter-billed birds.

Birds' legs and feet

In much the same way as the structure of a bird's bill tells us about its feeding habits, so the legs and feet provide information about its lifestyle. Anatomically, the part of a bird's lower limb that we call its 'leg' is formed of bones from the upper foot and is really equivalent to parts of our ankle, whereas the bones that are comparable to our lower and upper legs are hidden by feathers within the bird's flanks. In general, birds that possess short legs tend to hop, while those with long legs walk or run. Certain wading birds, such as cranes and herons, are characterised by unusually long legs that enable them to feed in deeper water without getting their plumage wet. The shortest legs are found in those birds that rarely walk, such as the Swift and Kingfisher.

Kingfishers have very short legs and rarely walk.

Similarly, the structure of the feet is adapted to the habitat in which each bird lives. Most land species have what would be considered to be typical bird's feet: long, widely separated toes, three pointing forwards and one back. This configuration, however, is not adopted in the woodpeckers, in which there are two toes pointing in each direction. This adaptation enables them to clamber more easily up the trunks and along the boughs. Such an arrangement is known as zygodactyl, from the Greek meaning 'yoke toed'.

By comparison, many water birds have webbed feet, the legs and feet being used as paddles when swimming. To further enhance propulsion, the legs in certain families, like the divers, are set further back on the body. In fact, they are set so far back that walking is virtually impossible. On land, a bird such as a Red-throated Diver has to wriggle along on its belly. Between these two extremes, grebes are provided with lobed toes, which are twisted sideways as the legs move forwards while swimming, in much the same way that an oarsman feathers his blades.

A woodpecker's feet are specially adapted to enable the bird to clamber up tree trunks.

Special adaptations in owls

Finally, perhaps some of the most interesting adaptations in birds are found in the owls, which may be described as cats with wings. While hunting they are prepared to wait silently and motionless for long periods before suddenly pouncing on their prey. They possess long, sharp claws, often hunt at night and at times can be incredibly noisy. So what are the special adaptations that enable owls to thrive so successfully in their strange twilight world?

One of the most striking features of an owl is its large, round, almost human-like face, and it is in the anatomy of the skull that many of its specialised characteristics are found. The majority of owls are nocturnal. Although it is not true that owls can see in total darkness, they do have to be able to hunt for their food under conditions of very low light. This is achieved by having comparatively large, forward-facing eyes, which provide excellent binocular vision. The ability to judge distance accurately is largely dependent on being able to focus on an object with both eyes simultaneously. One of the most endearing habits of owls is their head-bobbing action, another ploy to help them judge distance by viewing an object from different angles.

An owl's hearing is also particularly acute, another extremely valuable asset when hunting at night. Birds have no external ears as such, and in owls the sounds travel through large vertical openings on the sides of the skull to the internal organs of hearing. The openings are concealed by the feathers of the facial discs, behind which are fringes of short, stiff feathers carried on flaps that can be moved to scan around for sound. The 'ear' tufts found in certain species of owl have, in fact, nothing at all to do with the sense of hearing.

For their size and weight, owls have very broad and often comparatively long wings, enabling them to fly apparently effortlessly in a characteristically buoyant manner, avoiding the need for frequent flapping. Silent approach to their intended prey is also aided by their generally softer plumage and by the fine comb-like serrations along the leading edges of their flight feathers. Finally, their hooked, hawk-like bills and long, sharp claws are both adaptations to their predatory feeding habits, while their feathered legs and feet provide protection against any bites from their mammalian prey.

Owls are supremely adapted for their night-time activities.

★★ **Crossbill** *Loxia curvirostra*

| S | S | A | W | HEATH, WOOD

Fairly common resident and occasional passage migrant in varying numbers. **ID** Unpredictable and often elusive. Resembles and behaves like a small parrot but with crossed mandibles. Female greenish. Feeds acrobatically in conifers, sidling along branches and moving from twig to twig by using its bill. Highly gregarious. Presence often betrayed by falling pine cones. **VOICE** Distinct 'chip-chip' contact call. Song a mixture of trills, twitters and contact calls. **NEST** In conifer, often at a considerable height from ground.

male

male

★★ **Scottish Crossbill**
Loxia scotica

| S | S | A | W | HEATH, WOOD

Scarce resident in Scotland. **ID** Heavier bill than Crossbill; plumages similar. **VOICE** Very similar to Crossbill. **NEST** As Crossbill.

★ **Bullfinch** *Pyrrhula pyrrhula*

| S | S | A | W | FARM, GARDEN, SCRUB, WOOD

Very common resident. **ID** Retiring habits, presence often betrayed by flash of white rump as it flies away. Plump, rounded breast and bull neck. Female greyish-buff below. Pairs remain together throughout the year. **VOICE** Haunting, piping 'hoee' contact call. Weak, creaky song rarely heard. **NEST** In bush or shrub.

male

★ **Linnet** *Carduelis cannabina*

| S | S | A | W | FARM, HEATH, SCRUB

Very common resident and partial migrant.
ID Brown upperparts, warmer chestnut in male; primaries edged white, creating a diffuse, ill-defined pale wing panel in flight. Female streaky brown, lacking pink on breast. Flocks in winter and spring. **VOICE** Flight call a rapid twittering. Song a rather quiet, musical twittering delivered from the top of a bush. **NEST** In thick bush, often gorse, and frequently in loose colony.

male

★ **Redwing** *Turdus iliacus*

| S | S | A | W | FARM, GARDEN, PARK, WOOD

Rare breeder in Scotland; very common winter visitor from Fennoscandia and Iceland. **ID** Like Song Thrush but with white or creamy 'eyebrow', chestnut flanks and streaked not spotted breast. In flight, chestnut 'armpit' and underwing. Often in mixed flock with Fieldfares. **VOICE** A thin 'tseep' in flight, often heard at night on migration, especially in October. **NEST** In tree or shrub.

★★ **Waxwing** *Bombycilla garrulus*

| S | S | A | W | FARM, GARDEN

Scarce to fairly common but unpredictable winter visitor from N and E Europe. **ID** Rotund Starling-sized bird with a thick crest. Bright yellow tips to flight feathers and tail, and sealing-wax-red tips to secondaries, duller in female. Gregarious and approachable but always remains wary while feeding on berries or fruit, e.g. cotoneaster, rowan and pyracantha. **VOICE** Distinct ringing trill, likened to a small bell; once heard never forgotten.

male

★ **Linnet** *Carduelis cannabina*

| S | S | A | W | FARM, HEATH, SCRUB

Very common resident and partial migrant. **ID** Brown upperparts, warmer chestnut in male; primaries edged white. Female streaky brown, lacking pink on breast. Flocks in winter and spring. **VOICE** Flight call a rapid twittering. Song a rather quiet, musical twittering delivered from the top of a bush. **NEST** In thick bush, often gorse, frequently in loose colony.

male

★ **Lesser Redpoll** *Carduelis cabaret*

| S | S | A | W | HEATH, WOOD

Common but declining resident and partial migrant. **ID** Small, heavily streaked finch with red forehead, black bib and pale wing bars. Female lacks pink on breast. Usually seen in tops of birches or alders, in winter not infrequently in mixed flocks with Siskins. **VOICE** Rapid, high-pitched, metallic trill in flight. Song similar to flight calls, given from top of birch or in song flight. **NEST** Often high in tree or tall bush, usually in loose colony.

female

male

★★ **Common Redpoll** *Carduelis flammea*

| S | S | A | W | WOOD

Fairly common winter visitor from Scandinavia. **ID** Slightly larger than Lesser Redpoll; generally paler and greyer with white wing bars and whitish, streaked rump. Female lacks pink on breast. Formerly known as Mealy Redpoll.

female

male

★ **Goldfinch** *Carduelis carduelis*

| S | S | A | W | FARM, GARDEN, PARK, SCRUB, WOOD

Very common and increasing resident and partial migrant. **ID** Unusually pointed bill for a finch. Sexes very similar with bright yellow wing bars in flight, but male has more extensive red on face. Feeds on thistles and teasels. **VOICE** Cheerful, trisyllabic flight call 'swit, wit, wit'. Song a mixture of rapid trills and twitters, incorporating the flight call. **NEST** In crown of tree, often on thinner, outer branch.

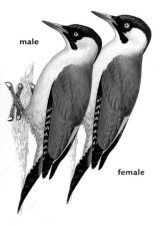

male

female

★ **Green Woodpecker** *Picus viridis*

| S | S | A | W | FARM, GARDEN, HEATH, PARK, WOOD

Common resident. **ID** Largest of our woodpeckers. Long, powerful, chisel-like bill; white iris; yellow rump visible in flight. Female lacks red stripe below the eye. Feeds on ground on ants and often deposits elongated, J-shaped grey droppings. Formerly known as Yaffle due to far-carrying, laughing call. **VOICE** Loud, ringing, rather hollow echoing calls in runs 'coo, co, coo...'. **NEST** In hole in tree.

★ **Great Spotted Woodpecker**
Dendrocopos major

| S | S | A | W | FARM, GARDEN, HEATH, PARK, WOOD

Common resident. **ID** Commonest and most widespread of our woodpeckers, a frequent visitor to garden bird feeders. Crown of female all black. Formerly known as Pied Woodpecker from large, white oval patches on upperparts. **VOICE** Sharp, penetrating 'kee, kee, kee...'. Drums in single rolls. **NEST** In hole in tree.

male

★★ **Lesser Spotted Woodpecker**
Dendrocopos minor

| S | S | A | W | FARM, PARK, WOOD

Fairly common but very localised and declining resident. **ID** Smallest and most sparsely distributed of our woodpeckers. Short, chisel-like bill; lacks red undertail coverts, compared with Great Spotted Woodpecker. Extensive red crown only in adult male, crown of female all black. Formerly known as Barred Woodpecker from white bars across black upperparts and wings. Tends to feed high in trees, foraging amongst the outermost, small branches. **VOICE** Similar 'kee' call to Great Spotted Woodpecker but quieter. Drumming carries for a shorter distance than Great Spotted and tends to be in two rolls in rapid succession. **NEST** In hole in tree.

male

★ Redstart *Phoenicurus phoenicurus*

| S | S | A | W | PARK, SCRUB, WOOD

Common summer visitor; fairly common passage migrant from Scandinavia, mainly in autumn. **ID** Slim with upright stance. Chestnut tail constantly quivered. Female brown above and buff below. Rarely seen on ground. **VOICE** Call an anxious 'wee-tik-tik' and thin 'wheet'. Short song, sweet, if slightly hoarse, rather like a Robin's with a terminal twitter. **NEST** In hole, generally in tree, but occasionally in wall or shed.

male

female

male

★ Stonechat *Saxicola torquatus*

| S | S | A | W | HEATH, MOOR, SCRUB

Common but declining resident and partial migrant. **ID** Plumper and more upright than Whinchat. Male much brighter than female, with black head and white half collar in breeding plumage. Often seen on top of bushes and fence posts, when it characteristically jerks wings and tail. **VOICE** Scolding 'wheest, tchack, tchack', like two stones being knocked together. Song rather quiet, short and scratchy, recalling Dunnock. **NEST** On or near ground in vegetation at base of bush.

★ Whinchat *Saxicola rubetra*

| S | S | A | W | FARM, HEATH, MOOR, SCRUB

Common summer visitor. **ID** Stocky; prominent pale 'eyebrow'; white patches at base of tail, which it often flicks. Male has blackish cheeks and white 'eyebrow' in breeding plumage. Flies low over ground. **VOICE** Scolding, sharp 'tic-tic'. Brief, clear, crisp song. **NEST** In tussock on ground, often at base of small bush.

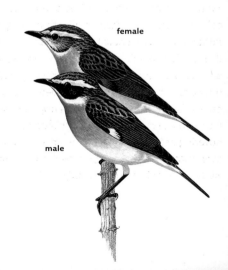

female

male

★ Chaffinch *Fringilla coelebs*

| S | S | A | W | FARM, GARDEN, HEATH, PARK, WOOD

Abundant resident and winter visitor mainly from Scandinavia. **ID** One of our most widespread birds and the second commonest. Double white wing bars and white sides to tail. Female uniformly buff. In winter sexes often found in separate flocks. **VOICE** Cheerful 'spink' and a difficult to locate 'hooeet'. Song a vigorous cascade with a terminal flourish, tirelessly repeated after a short interval and often followed by a nearby rival's song. **NEST** In fork of tree or bush.

male

★★ Hawfinch
Coccothraustes coccothraustes

| S | S | A | W | PARK, WOOD

Fairly common but localised resident. **ID** A large finch with a very powerful, heavy bill. Strange club-shaped extensions on inner primaries. In flight prominent white tip to tail and white wing bar. Often found in vicinity of hornbeams Very wary and despite flocking in winter can be extremely elusive. **VOICE** A Robin-like 'tzic'. **NEST** On horizontal branch of tree at varying height, often in loose colony of a few pairs.

★★ Kingfisher *Alcedo atthis*

| S | S | A | W | FRESH

Fairly common resident. **ID** One of our most colourful birds, but often smaller than imagined; rather dumpy and short tailed with a long, dagger-shaped bill. Sexes similar but male has all-black bill throughout year. Perches upright, but despite bright colours can be remarkably well camouflaged when sitting in shadow; plunges into water to catch small fish, occasionally hovering before diving; flies like an arrow low over water. **VOICE** A piping, metallic 'tzi' in flight. **NEST** In tunnelled hole in sandy bank.

★ **Nuthatch** *Sitta europaea*

| S | S | A | W | GARDEN, PARK, WOOD

Very common resident. **ID** Rather dumpy and short-tailed, with a dagger-like bill; chestnut flanks brighter on male. Our only bird able to climb down tree trunks headfirst. **VOICE** A variety of calls and songs, including a loud, ringing, oft-repeated 'chwit-chwit-chwit' and a shrill trill. **NEST** In hole in tree, with mud plastered around entrance hole and any crevices in cavity.

★ **Robin** *Erithacus rubecula*

| S | S | A | W | FARM, GARDEN, WOOD

Abundant resident; fairly common passage migrant from N Europe, mainly in autumn. **ID** One of our most familiar birds, aided by its appearance on Christmas cards. **VOICE** A short, sharp 'tic'. Song consists of a collection of rather thin notes, varying in volume and speed. One of the few birds to sing throughout the winter; also on occasion sings at night by the light of a street lamp, when it may be mistaken for a Nightingale. **NEST** Well concealed in hollow on bank, or in cavity in tree stump, wall or thick scrub.

male breeding

★★★ **Red-breasted Flycatcher**
Ficedula parva

| S | S | A | W | SCRUB, WOOD

Rare visitor from NE Europe to coastal areas. **ID** Our smallest flycatcher. Narrow white eye ring; broad white base to dark tail feathers, especially noticeable as bird flies away. Female lacks red breast of summer-plumaged male. Very restless, constantly on move, feeding warbler-like in canopy, but occasionally sits still on perch, when it flicks tail and droops wings. **VOICE** Quiet, Wren-like chatter and sharp 'chik'.

★★★ **Bluethroat** *Luscinia svecica*

| S | s | **A** | w | SCRUB |

Red-spotted male breeding

Rare visitor from continental Europe to coastal areas. **ID** Whitish 'eyebrow'; chestnut at base of tail, especially visible in flight. Variable amount of blue in autumn. Actions much as Robin; flicks tail when perched. Two races: Red-spotted (*L.s.svecica*) from N Europe and White-spotted (*L.s.cyanecula*) from S and Central Europe. **VOICE** A sharp 'tac'.

★★ **Brambling** *Fringilla montifringilla*

| S | s | **A** | **W** | FARM, GARDEN, WOOD |

Occasional breeder in Scotland; common winter visitor, mainly from Fennoscandia. **ID** Size and shape of Chaffinch; orange tinge at least to breast in all plumages, with dark, round spots on flanks; rump white. Head greyish-brown in female. Associates with Chaffinches; often found feeding on beech mast in winter. **VOICE** Loud, harsh, questioning 'tchweep' and quiet 'tchup'.

female breeding

male breeding

★ **Blackcap** *Sylvia atricapilla*

| **S** | **S** | **A** | **W** | FARM, GARDEN, WOOD |

Very common summer visitor and scarce winter visitor from Central Europe. **ID** Female greyish-brown above and paler below, with a chestnut cap. **VOICE** Call a hard 'tac, tac', louder than Lesser Whitethroat Song a rich, fluty warble, more varied but less sustained than Garden Warbler. **NEST** Above ground in low bush, brambles, evergreen or other woody vegetation.

female

★ **Yellowhammer** *Emberiza citrinella*

| **S** | **S** | **A** | **W** | FARM, HEATH, SCRUB |

Abundant but declining resident. **ID** Chestnut rump and conspicuous white outer tail feathers visible on flying away. Female duller and more streaked. Often perches conspicuously on top of bush, tree or wires. **VOICE** Flight call a single, metallic 'chip' or double 'pit, pit'. Song the familiar 'a little bit of bread and no cheeeese'. **NEST** Well concealed in grass or vegetation at base of hedge or on side of overgrown bank.

male

★★ **Cetti's Warbler** *Cettia cetti*

| S | S | A | **W** | FRESH, REEDS, SCRUB

Scarce but increasing resident of lowland river valleys. **ID** Far more often heard than seen. Rather plump, short-necked warbler with broad, rounded tail, often held partly raised; short, whitish 'eyebrow'; white eye ring around lower lid. Skulks low down in undergrowth like a mouse. **VOICE** Sudden, short, explosive song, incorporating 'cetti, cetti'. **NEST** Low down in thick herbage.

female

male

★★ **Bearded Tit**
Panurus biarmicus

| S | S | A | W | REEDS

Scarce resident and partial migrant. **ID** Lives exclusively in or near reedbeds. Tawny brown bird with a long tail, hence old colloquial name of 'Reed Pheasant'. Female lacks blue head and black moustache, bill usually dark. Whirring flight across tops of reeds, but remains low down in reeds on windy days. **VOICE** Distinct twanging or pinging calls, given at rest and in flight. **NEST** Low down in reeds, near edge of stand.

★ **Linnet** *Carduelis cannabina*

| S | S | A | W | FARM, HEATH, SCRUB

Very common resident and partial migrant. **ID** Brown upperparts, warmer chestnut in male; primaries edged white creating a diffuse, ill-defined pale wing panel in flight. Female streaky brown, lacking pink on breast. Flocks in winter and spring. **VOICE** Flight call a rapid twittering. Song a rather quiet, musical twittering delivered from the top of a bush. **NEST** In thick bush, often gorse, and frequently in loose colony.

male

★ **Whitethroat** *Sylvia communis*

| S | S | A | W | FARM, HEATH, SCRUB |

Very common summer visitor. **ID** As name implies, has distinct white throat, which contrasts with grey head of male; broad chestnut area on closed wing; straw-coloured legs; tail often cocked. A restless bird, darting in and out of cover. **VOICE** Hoarse, scolding 'tchair'. Song an oft-repeated brief, scratchy chattering, given during dancing song flight or from top of bush. **NEST** In low shrub or tall plants, e.g. nettles, about 30cm off ground.

★ **Fieldfare** *Turdus pilaris*

| S | S | A | W | FARM, MOOR, PARK, WOOD |

Rare breeder and abundant winter visitor from N Europe. **ID** Appears larger than Blackbird, having longer wings and tail. In flight pale grey rump and white underwing (like Mistle Thrush). Gregarious and often associates with Redwings and Starlings. Dive-bombs and defecates on intruders in breeding territory. **VOICE** Flight calls a chattering 'tchak, tchak, tchak' and a quieter 'see'. Song a brief, simple chattering. **NEST** In fork of tree, usually in loose colony.

★★★ **Red-backed Shrike**
Lanius collurio

| S | S | A | W | HEATH, SCRUB |

Rare summer visitor and passage migrant from N Europe. **ID** Perches in open but can be surprisingly elusive. Female dull rufous-brown above and barred below. When perched, often swings tail from side to side; tail appears fairly long in flight. **VOICE** Harsh, grating 'check'. **NEST** In bush or shrub.

male

★ **Nightingale** *Luscinia megarhynchos*

| S | S | A | W | HEATH, SCRUB, WOOD

Fairly common but declining summer visitor. **ID** An elusive bird that is far more often heard than seen. Featureless, except for bright chestnut rump and tail; pale eye ring in otherwise plain face. **VOICE** Its famous song is loud and musical, with each rounded, full-bodied note being repeated several times; may sing continuously for several minutes. Characteristic notes include a liquid 'wheet', bubbling 'chook-chook-chook' and 'pew-pew-pew' rising in a crescendo. **NEST** Well concealed on or near ground under shrubs.

female

male

★ **Redstart** *Phoenicurus phoenicurus*

| S | S | A | W | PARK, SCRUB, WOOD

Common summer visitor; fairly common passage migrant from Scandinavia, mainly in autumn. **ID** Slim and upright stance. Chestnut tail constantly quivered. Rarely seen on ground. **VOICE** Call an anxious 'wee-tik-tik' and thin 'wheet'. Short song sweet, if slightly hoarse, rather like a Robin's with a terminal twitter. **NEST** In hole, generally in tree, but occasionally in wall or shed.

★★ **Black Redstart** *Phoenicurus ochruros*

| S | S | A | W | BUILDINGS, COAST

female

Rare breeder; scarce winter visitor and passage migrant from Europe. **ID** Often very elusive. Constantly quivering bright chestnut tail. Usually seen perched on building or fence, from where it drops to feed briefly on ground. **VOICE** Scolding 'tucc-tucc' and snappy 'fist'. Short, loud, warbling song with terminal flourish. **NEST** In recess or hole in building, at sites such as power stations, gas works, railway sheds or derelict industrial areas.

male

★★★ **Bluethroat** *Luscinia svecica*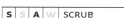

| S | s | A | w | SCRUB

Rare visitor from continental Europe to coastal areas. **ID** Whitish 'eyebrow'; chestnut at base of tail, especially visible in flight. Only adult males have significant area of blue on throat. Actions much as Robin; flicks tail when perched. Two races: Red-spotted (*L.s.svecica*) from N Europe and White-spotted (*L.s.cyanecula*) from S and Central Europe. **VOICE** A sharp 'tac'.

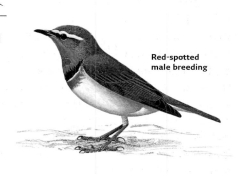

Red-spotted male breeding

female

male

★ **Yellowhammer**
Emberiza citrinella

| S | s | A | W | FARM, HEATH, SCRUB

Abundant but declining resident. **ID** Chestnut rump and conspicuous white outer tail feathers visible on flying away. Male has bright yellow head and underparts. Often perches conspicuously on top of bush, tree or wires. **VOICE** Flight call a single, metallic 'chip' or double 'pit, pit'. Song the familiar 'a little bit of bread and no cheeeese'. **NEST** Well concealed in grass or vegetation at base of hedge or on side of overgrown bank.

★ Jay *Garrulus glandarius*

| S | S | A | W | FARM, GARDEN, PARK, WOOD

Very common resident. **ID** Bright blue wing patch finely barred black; white rump. Raises crown feathers in alarm or display. Often moves around in small, noisy parties. **VOICE** Loud and raucous 'tchaar'. A great mimic; song comprises a bizarre mixture of clicks, mews and chuckles. **NEST** In fork against main trunk of tree.

★★★ Hoopoe *Upupa epops*

| S | S | A | W | FARM, GARDEN, HEATH, PARK

Rare passage migrant from Europe. **ID** Unmistakable, pinkish-buff bird with black and white bars across wings; long, erectile black and white crest; long, thin, decurved bill. Broadly rounded wings with characteristic unculating, floppy flight. Feeds on ground, often on areas of short grass. **VOICE** Far-carrying, hollow-sounding 'poo, poo, poo'.

★ Turtle Dove
Streptopelia turtur

| S | S | A | W | FARM, SCRUB, WOOD

Common but declining summer visitor to England and Wales. **ID** Smallest and slimmest of our doves. Bright orange on closed wing; striped black and white neck patch; broad white tail tip conspicuous in flight. Often seen in pairs. **VOICE** Gentle purring. **NEST** In bush, hedgerow or small tree.

★ Feral Pigeon
Columba livia

|S|S|A|W| BUILDINGS, COAST, FARM

Very common resident. **ID** Occurs in a wide variety of plumages from white through grey to almost black, as well as pink (known as Red Chequer or Mealy). Majority lack white rump. **VOICE** Familiar cooing. **NEST** Often colonial on ledges on or in buildings.

pink variety

★★★ Rose-coloured Starling
Sturnus roseus

|S|S|A|W| FARM, GARDEN

Rare visitor from E Europe and Asia. **ID** Pink and black adult is unmistakable. Compared with Starling, juvenile is rather paler with darker, more contrasting wings, a pale rump and shorter, yellowish bill. Size and behaviour as Starling, with which it usually associates. **VOICE** As Starling.

★★★ Water Pipit *Anthus spinoletta*

|S|S|A|W| COAST, FRESH, MARSH

Rare winter visitor from S Europe. **ID** In breeding plumage has grey head and pinkish tinge to breast and can be confused with Scandinavian race of Rock Pipit (*A.p.littoralis*). In winter very similar to Rock Pipit but paler underparts, whiter 'eyebrow', white wing bars and white outer tail feathers. Unlike Rock Pipit, favours inland wetland sites, especially watercress beds. **VOICE** Flight call a single, thin 'tseep', compared with short run of notes given by Meadow Pipit.

breeding

★ **Lesser Redpoll** *Carduelis*

male

S | S | A | W HEATH, WOOD

Common but declining resident and partial migrant.
ID Small, heavily streaked finch with red forehead,
black bib and pale wing bars. Female lacks pink on
breast. Usually seen in tops of birches or alders, in
winter not infrequently in mixed flocks with Siskins.
VOICE Rapid, high-pitched, metallic trill in flight. Song
similar to flight calls, given from top of birch or in
song flight. **NEST** Often high in tree or tall bush,
usually in loose colony.

male

★★ **Common Redpoll**
Carduelis flammea

S | S | A | W WOOD

Fairly common winter visitor from Fennoscandia.
ID Slightly larger than Lesser Redpoll; generally
paler and greyer with white wing bars and
whitish, streaked rump. Female lacks pink on
breast. Formerly known as Mealy Redpoll.

★★ **Twite** *Carduelis flavirostris*

S | S | A | W COAST, HEATH, MOOR, MOUNTAIN

Localised resident and partial migrant. **ID** Very
similar to female Linnet with few distinguishing
features, but more streaky and warmer buff with less
white in wing; yellow bill in winter. Female lacks pink
rump. Forms dense winter flocks. **VOICE** Call a
diagnostic nasal 'tzweet' included in constant
twittering in flight. Song fast trills and buzzing notes.
NEST On open ground amongst low cover.

male breeding

male

★ **Whitethroat** *Sylvia communis*

| S | S | A | w | FARM, HEATH, SCRUB

Very common summer visitor. **ID** As name implies, has distinct white throat, particularly noticeable in singing or displaying male; broad chestnut area on closed wing; straw-coloured legs; tail often cocked. Male pinkish below, female buff. A restless bird, darting in and out of cover. **VOICE** Hoarse, scolding 'tchair'. Song an oft-repeated brief, scratchy chattering, given during dancing song flight or from top of bush. **NEST** In low shrub or tall plants, e.g. nettles, about 30cm off ground.

★★ **Dartford Warbler**
Sylvia undata

| S | S | A | W | HEATH

Fairly common but very localised resident. **ID** Elusive and skulking. A generally dark bird, grey above and dull wine-red below; long, graduated tail usually cocked. Female duller. Rapid, whirring flight on short wings. Usually found amongst gorse or heather. Often associates with Stonechat. **VOICE** A Wren-like scolding churr and rattle. Song a musical chatter recalling Whitethroat. **NEST** In scrub near ground.

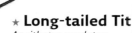

male

★ **Long-tailed Tit**
Aegithalos caudatus

<

| S | S | A | W | FARM, GARDEN, HEATH, WOOD

Very common resident. **ID** Easily recognised by small size and long tail. Acrobatic while feeding, usually in pairs or family parties that remain together throughout winter. **VOICE** Constant, noisy trilling calls and thin 'tsee-tsee-tsee'. **NEST** Domed nest built of moss and lichen in thick bush, such as gorse or bramble, or in conifer.

★ Sparrowhawk *Accipiter nisus*

male

| S | S | A | W | FARM, GARDEN, MARSH, PARK, WOOD

Common resident; fairly common winter visitor, mainly from Scancinavia. **ID** Nowadays almost as common as Kestrel. Long, thin, yellow legs visible when perched. Female larger than male with brownish-grey barring below. In fl ght short, rounded wings and longish, barred, square-cornered tail. Low-level, hedge-hopping flight to surprise potential victims; also pigeon-like flight with a few flaps followed by a glide. Infrequently perches out in open. **VOICE** Loud and rapid 'kek, kek, kek' **NEST** At variable height in tree, sometimes in an old nest of another species.

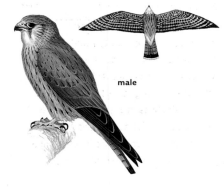

male

★★ Merlin *Falco columbarius*

| S | S | A | W | COAST, FARM, HEATH, MARSH, MOOR

Fairly common but localised breeder and partial migrant. **ID** The small, dashing falcon of open country that recalls a miniature Peregrine. Indistinct stripe below the eye. Female brownish-grey above, paler below; broadly barred tail. In flight rapid wing beats and occasional glides. **VOICE** Rapid 'ki-ki-ki-ki'. **NEST** Usually on ground in open moorland.

★★ Hobby *Falco subbuteo*

| S | S | A | W | FARM, FRESH, HEATH, MOOR

Scarce summer visitor. **ID** Contrasting white throat and black stripe below the eye; chestnut feathering on thighs and undertail coverts. In flight long, pointed, swept-back wings. Dashing, swift-like flight enables it to take birds and insects in the air. **VOICE** A scolding 'kew, kew, kew, kew.' **NEST** In tree in the nest of another larger bird or on a squirrel drey.

★ Kestrel *Falco tinnunculus*

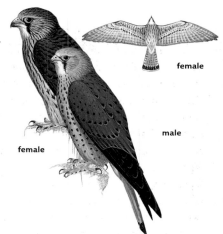

| S | S | A | W | FARM, HEATH, MOOR, PARK, WOOD

Common resident and partial migrant. **ID** Generally the most familiar bird of prey, readily identified by its hovering flight. Reddish-brown above with darker flight feathers. Male has blue-grey head and tail, female brown head and tail, barred darker. In flight long, pointed wings and tail; only occasionally glides but frequently hovers with tail spread. Often seen perched on tree or telegraph pole. **VOICE** Shrill 'kee, kee, kee'. **NEST** On ledge or in a cavity of a cliff, building or tree.

★★ Red Kite *Milvus milvus*

| S | S | A | W | FARM, MOOR, PARK, WOOD

Scarce but increasing resident, aided by recent re-introduction programmes; rare spring migrant from Europe. **ID** Large, long-winged raptor with long, deeply forked chestnut tail. Effortless, buoyant flight with wings arched and swept backwards from mid-wing; uses tail as rudder. **VOICE** Buzzard-like mewing. **NEST** At variable height in tree.

★★ Marsh Harrier
Circus aeruginosus

| S | S | A | W | FARM, MARSH, REEDS

Scarce but increasing resident and summer visitor. **ID** Narrower wings and longer tail than Common Buzzard, but broader wings than other harriers. Male has contrasting grey, brown and black wings; female has a distinctly pale head and paler leading edge to inner wing. Rather lazy, low, quartering flight; also soars high in air with wings raised in shallow V. **NEST** On platform of dead vegetation in reedbed or on ground amongst cereal or arable crop.

★★ Golden Pheasant
Chrysolophus pictus

| S | S | A | W | WOOD

Scarce and declining introduced resident, mainly found in E Anglia. **ID** Secretive and elusive despite bright colours of male. Very long, pointed tail. Female like Pheasant but proportionately longer tail and dark bars, not spots. **VOICE** Deer-like shriek, higher pitched than Pheasant, recalling a quiet or distant Jay. **NEST** On ground in thick cover.

male

★ Pheasant *Phasianus colchicus*

| S | S | A | W | FARM, MARSH, PARK, WOOD

Abundant resident. **ID** Commonest and most familiar game bird. Very long, pointed tail. Female buffy-brown with darker spots. Some males have white collar and a grey rump (*P.c.torquatus*) formerly known as the Ring-necked Pheasant; others lacking the white collar and having a brown rump (*P.c.colchicus*) were formerly known as the Old English Pheasant. A dark green hybrid ('*tenebrosus*') is also becoming increasingly widespread in E Anglia. Runs rapidly to cover rather than taking off, but when it does so is noisy with whirring wings. **VOICE** Male gives familiar 'kok, kok'. **NEST** On ground in long grass or amongst tallish vegetation or shrubs.

Ring-necked male

Old English male

male

★ Grey Partridge *Perdix perdix*

S S A W FARM

Very common but declining resident. **ID** Rotund, chicken-like bird with small head and very short neck. Smaller than Red-legged Partridge; both species have reddish tail. Female less brightly marked with smaller belly patch. Flies low with whirring wing beats and short, stiff-winged glides. **VOICE** When flushed an excited 'krri, krri, krri'. Song rather hoarse 'kieerric', with accent on last syllable. **NEST** On ground in tall grass, vegetation or crops.

★ Red-legged Partridge
Alectoris rufa

S S A W FARM, HEATH, PARK, SCRUB

Very common resident. **ID** Slightly larger than Grey Partridge and has white face, a necklace of black streaks and bold barring on flanks. In flight lower back and rump grey compared with brown of Grey Partridge, but tends to run away rather than taking flight. Gregarious, groups of partridges being known as 'coveys'. **VOICE** Distinctive 'chukar', often repeated several times. **NEST** On ground, usually among growing plants and often in shelter of a bush.

★★★ Corncrake *Crex crex*

S S A W FARM, MARSH

Localised summer visitor to N and W Isles and Ireland. **ID** Far more often heard than seen. A slim bird but with a rounded body. Heavily spotted above, barred on flanks and undertail coverts; chestnut inner wings conspicuous in flight. Crepuscular and very elusive, slipping away on foot rather than taking flight. **VOICE** Rasping, coarse 'crex, crex'. May be imitated by dragging plastic credit card across teeth of a comb. **NEST** Hidden amongst thick ground vegetation or crops.

★★★ Red-necked Phalarope
Phalaropus lobatus

| S | S | A | W | COAST, FRESH, MARSH

Rare summer visitor to N Isles; elsewhere scarce passage migrant to coasts and inland pools. **ID** Smaller and daintier than Grey Phalarope with very fine, all-black bill. Unmistakable in breeding plumage. Often very tame, feeds by wading as well as by spinning on surface of water. Female more brightly coloured than male during breeding season. **NEST** In poolside tussock.

female breeding

★★ Ruff *Philomachus pugnax*

| S | S | A | W | FARM, MARSH

Rare breeder in England; scarce passage migrant and winter visitor from Europe, mainly to coastal marshes in S and E. **ID** Males (Ruffs) up to size of Redshank but bulkier, some females (Reeves) almost as small as Dunlin but longer neck and legs. Small head on longish neck; medium length, slightly decurved bill; leg colour varies from orangey-red through yellow to greenish; upperparts scalloped. In breeding plumage males' ruff and ear tufts vary from rufous or orange to black or white, and are raised and lowered at communal display grounds known as 'leks'. Female and non-breeding male have distinctly scaly upperparts. Often feed on flooded fields. **NEST** Concealed amongst ground vegetation on grassy or marshy areas.

male breeding

★ Knot *Calidris canutus*

| S | S | A | W | COAST

Very common but localised winter visitor from the Arctic, mainly to the larger estuaries. **ID** A dumpy wader, larger and stockier than Dunlin; rather short, thickish, straight bill; shortish legs. Largely grey in winter. Forms massive, dense, roosting flocks at high tide; when disturbed, birds fly in close formation, creating a smoke-like effect. **VOICE** Flight call a disyllabic 'kwip, kwip'.

breeding

★★ Curlew Sandpiper
Calidris ferruginea

`S` | `S` | `A` | `W` | MARSH

Scarce visitor from Arctic Siberia, mainly to coastal marshes in autumn. **ID** Slightly larger, longer necked and more upright than Dunlin, with longer, more decurved bill and longer legs. Pale grey in winter. **VOICE** Flight call a very distinctive, liquid 'chirrip'.

breeding

★ Bar-tailed Godwit
Limosa lapponica

`S` | `S` | `A` | `W` | COAST

Common winter visitor from Arctic Russia and Siberia to flat coastal areas. **ID** Appears smaller than Black-tailed Godwit due to shorter legs; dark bill long and slightly upcurved; barred tail not always easy to see. In breeding plumage, compared with Black-tailed Godwit, lacks barring on underparts and chestnut extends to under tail. In winter Curlew-like brownish-grey upperparts streaked darker. **VOICE** Flight call a sharp 'keewick'.

male breeding

★★ Black-tailed Godwit
Limosa limosa

`S` | `S` | `A` | `W` | COAST, MARSH

Rare breeder in England; fairly common winter visitor and passage migrant from Iceland. **ID** Tall, slim wader; longer, straighter, orange-based bill and longer upper legs than Bar-tailed Godwit. In winter uniform buffy-grey. Outside breeding season often found in large flocks. **VOICE** Lapwing-like flight call and oft-repeated 'wicka-wicka-wicka...' in display flight. **NEST** On ground in lush vegetation on grassy meadow or marshland.

breeding

breeding

★★★ Dotterel *Charadrius morinellus*

| S | S | A | W | COAST, FARM, MOUNTAIN

Summer visitor to mountains in N, mainly the Scottish Highlands; rare passage migrant elsewhere. **ID** Smaller and squatter than Golden Plover; long pale 'eyebrow' and dark crown. In non-breeding plumage greyish-buff underparts. Female more brightly coloured than male during breeding season. **VOICE** Flight call a soft, rolling trill. **NEST** Shallow hollow on ground on mountain top.

★ Turnstone *Arenaria interpres*

| S | S | A | W | COAST

Common winter visitor from the Arctic, mainly to rocky coasts. **ID** Stocky wader with shortish, wedge-shaped bill and orange legs. In winter dark above and white below. Searches for food by flipping over pebbles, seaweed, etc. **VOICE** Flight call a metallic, staccato 'tuk-a-tuk'.

breeding

★ Dunlin *Calidris alpina*

| S | S | A | W | COAST, MARSH, MOOR, MOUNTAIN

Fairly common, mainly upland breeder; very common coastal passage migrant and winter visitor from Greenland, Iceland and N Europe. **ID** The most abundant shore wader in winter, often found in large flocks. Length of bill varies according to sex and race, with longest billed breeding in Arctic. Black belly in breeding plumage. In winter grey above and white below. **VOICE** Flight call a rolling 'treee'. **NEST** On ground in grassy tussock.

breeding

breeding

★ **Sanderling** *Calidris alba*

| S | S | A | W | COAST

Fairly common winter visitor from Siberia to sandy coasts. **ID** Small, strikingly pale wader in winter, characteristic of open sandy beaches; rather short, stout bill. In breeding plumage, rufous upper breast sharply demarcated from white underparts. In winter pale grey. Runs back and forth following the ebb and flow of the waves. **VOICE** Flight call a liquid 'quit-quit'.

★★ **Little Stint** *Calidris minute*

| S | S | A | W | COAST, MARSH

Scarce passage migrant, mainly in autumn, from Arctic Norway and Siberia; rare but regular in winter. **ID** Smallest of the common waders, often found in flocks with Dunlin. Dainty; pale V on back; short straight bill; legs black. Rufous markings present only in breeding plumage. In winter grey above and white below. More rapid feeding action than Dunlin. **VOICE** Shrill, high-pitched 'tit'.

breeding

breeding

★ **Lapwing** *Vanellus vanellus*

| S | S | A | W | COAST, FARM, MARSH

Very common but decreasing lowland breeder; abundant winter visitor from N Europe. **ID** One of the characteristic birds of farmland. Appears black and white, but upperparts have greeny purple iridescence; long, thin, wispy crest; orange vent most visible when the bird tips forward to feed. Tumbling display flight in spring. Often in large flocks out of breeding season. Also known as Peewit or Green Plover. **VOICE** Scolding 'peewee'. **NEST** On ground on field or marshland.

★★★ Ruddy Shelduck
Tadorna ferruginea

s | s | A | w FARM, MARSH

Rare visitor from SE Europe and Asia; most seen are feral birds. **ID** Goose-like duck with head distinctly paler than body. Male black ring around neck in summer, female white face mask. Closely related Cape Shelduck has different-coloured head: grey in drake and black and white in female.

female

male

★★ Egyptian Goose *Alopochen aegyptiaca*

s | s | A | w FARM, FRESH, MARSH, PARK

Scarce introduced resident mainly found in E Anglia. **ID** Strange, pinkish-brown bird with dark face mask giving it a roguish appearance; females less strongly marked than males. **VOICE** Loud, husky wheezing calls, given both in flight and on ground. **NEST** In hole in tree.

★ Wigeon *Anas penelope*

s | s | A | w FRESH, MARSH

Scarce breeder mainly in N; very common winter visitor from N Europe and Siberia. **ID** Eclipse (post-breeding) drake richer colour than female, with white belly and white wing panel in flight. Head of drake chestnut with pale yellow central crown stripe in breeding plumage. A grazing duck, often forming large winter flocks and joining Brent Geese on coastal saltings and marshes. **VOICE** Drake gives characteristic drawn-out whistle. **NEST** On ground in thick waterside vegetation.

male eclipse

female

★★ Ruddy Duck *Oxyura jamaicensis*

s | s | A | w FRESH

Native American species that spread following escape from Slimbridge in 1957, now a scarce resident, mainly in the Midlands. **ID** Small and compact with a longish tail, often cocked (thus known as a 'stiff tail'). Drake has pale blue bill in breeding plumage. Female dark brown with paler cheek. Gives small leap before diving to feed or escape danger. **NEST** On floating platform in dense aquatic vegetation.

male breeding

★★ **Mandarin** *Aix galericulata*

| S | S | **A** | **W** | FRESH, PARK, WOOD

Scarce resident feral population mainly in S.
ID Breeding plumage of drake the most
spectacular and unmistakable of any British
duck. Female grey-brown with white spectacles.
In flight streamlined shape with uniformly dark
upperwings. **NEST** In hole in tree.

male

male breeding

★ **Shoveler** *Anas clypeata*

| S | S | **A** | **W** | FRESH

Fairly common resident; winter visitor from
N Europe. **ID** Both sexes characterised by large,
spatulate bill with which they skim the water
surface for food. Drake's head can look black at
distance. Female all brown. Usually seen in pairs
or small, dense, circling groups when feeding.
NEST Hollow in low waterside vegetation.

★ **Shelduck** *Tadorna tadorna*

| S | S | **A** | **W** | COAST, FARM, FRESH, HEATH, MARSH

Common resident around coasts and estuaries, also
breeding inland. **ID** One of the most conspicuous
and colourful estuarine birds; can appear black and
white at a distance. Drake larger and more brightly
coloured with broader breast band and brighter red
knob above bill. **VOICE** Drake gives characteristic
hissing whistle in flight, female a nagging, guttural
call. **NEST** Usually in underground burrow.

female

male

★★★ Red-crested Pochard *Netta rufina*

| S | S | A | W | FRESH

Genuine wild birds are rare visitors from S and E Europe; small numbers of feral birds breed mainly in S and E. **ID** One of the largest freshwater diving ducks. Drake's brightly coloured head and red bill make it unmistakable. Female a rather bland, washed-out plain pale brown with dark crown and pale cheeks, recalling a large female Common Scoter.

male

★ Pochard *Aythya ferina*

| S | S | A | W | FRESH

Scarce breeder; common winter visitor from Central Europe. **ID** Distinctive peaked crown and sloping forehead forming sweeping curve along top of bill, which in drake has grey band. Female fairly uniform pale grey-brown. Gregarious diving duck, rarely found alone. **NEST** Pile of plant material in waterside vegetation.

male

★ Wigeon *Anas penelope*

| S | S | A | W | FRESH, MARSH

Scarce breeder mainly in N; very common winter visitor from N Europe and Siberia. **ID** Drake shows yellow central crown stripe and white wing patch in flight. Female has variable chestnut underparts. Grazing ducks often form large winter flocks and join Brent Geese on coastal saltings and marshes. **VOICE** Drake gives characteristic drawn-out whistle. **NEST** On ground in thick waterside vegetation.

male

★ Teal *Anas crecca*

| S | S | A | W | FRESH, MARSH

Fairly common breeder in N and W; very common winter visitor from N Europe and Siberia. **ID** Our smallest duck. Drake has horizontal white stripe along flank and green eye patch outlined in yellow. Female all brown. Feeds by upending and leaps from water on taking off, hence the collective noun a 'spring' of Teal. **VOICE** Very vocal when displaying in groups, giving a high-pitched, chirruping call. **NEST** Well concealed in ground vegetation.

male

★ **Goosander** *Mergus merganser*

| S | S | A | W | FRESH |

Fairly common breeder on rivers and inland waters in N and W, spreading further south in winter. **ID** Large, long, heavy body; long red bill with hooked tip. Female has distinct crest and sharp division between chestnut head and grey neck. Drake has dark green head and white underparts with a pink flush in winter. Feeds by diving, often in groups. **NEST** In hole in tree, bank or amongst boulders near water.

female

★ **Red-breasted Merganser**
Mergus serrator

| S | S | A | W | COAST, FRESH |

Fairly common breeder in freshwater and tidal habitats in N and W, moving to coastal waters in winter. **ID** Smaller and slimmer than Goosander; shaggy crest; finer bill. In female chestnut of head 'merges' into grey neck. Drake has dark green head and brown breast. Feeds by diving. **NEST** Concealed under vegetation or boulder near water.

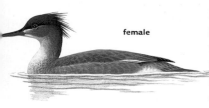

female

★★ **Smew** *Mergellus albellus* < Mallard

<

| S | S | A | W | FRESH |

Scarce winter visitor from NE Europe and Siberia to inland waters. **ID** Female and immature drakes small and compact, known as 'red heads'. Adult drake very distinct, mainly white. Feeds by diving, often in shallowish water. Lone birds are usually rather shy, tending to feed near aquatic vegetation amongst which they can readily hide.

female

★ Great Crested Grebe
Podiceps cristatus

>

| S | S | A | W | COAST, FRESH

Fairly common and widespread resident of lowland waters. **ID** Largest, slimmest and most elegant grebe; long slender neck and bill; ornate head plumes in breeding plumage. Appears predominantly black and white in winter. Breeding pairs engage in head-turning displays. **NEST** On mound of aquatic vegetation near water's edge.

breeding

★★ Red-necked Grebe
Podiceps grisegena

>

breeding

| S | S | A | W | COAST, FRESH

Scarce winter visitor from NE Europe to coastal waters, mainly in S and E, with a few inland. **ID** Rarely seen in full breeding plumage in Britain and Ireland. In winter shows dark cheeks and some chestnut on neck. Leaps up before diving.

★★ Black-necked Grebe
Podiceps nigricollis

breeding

| S | S | A | W | COAST, FRESH

Rare breeder; scarce winter visitor to coastal and inland waters mainly in S and W. **ID** Steep forehead and peak of crown above eye; fine uptilted bill; fluffed-out rear end. In winter black above and white below. Often elusive, disappearing into dense reeds. **NEST** On low mound of waterside vegetation.

★★ Slavonian Grebe *Podiceps auritus*

| S | S | A | W | COAST, FRESH

Rare breeder, mainly in Scotland; scarce winter visitor to coastal waters. **ID** In breeding plumage, a most beautiful bird with golden tufts on top of head; short straight bill with pale tip. In winter black above and white below. The most maritime of our grebes in winter. **NEST** On floating mound of vegetation in shallow water.

breeding

★ **Little Grebe** *Tachybaptus ruficollis*

| S | S | A | W | FRESH

Common and widespread resident of lowland waters. **ID** Smallest and dumpiest grebe; short neck and bill; fluffed-up rear end. Chestnut cheeks and neck in breeding plumage, which become pale buff in winter. Swims buoyantly, but if disturbed may submerge, leaving only head showing, or may dive and disappear amongst waterside vegetation. **VOICE** High-pitched trills given by pair in unison. **NEST** Amongst waterside vegetation.

breeding

★ **Red-throated Diver**
Gavia stellata

| S | S | A | W | COAST, FRESH

Fairly common but localised breeder in Scotland; common winter visitor to coastal waters. **ID** Commonest, smallest and slimmest diver; bill uptilted and held pointing skywards. In breeding plumage, deep red velvet throat patch can look black at distance; vertical black and white stripes on back of neck. Appears predominantly black and white in winter. **NEST** Shallow scrape on mound by shore.

breeding

★★★ **Red-necked Phalarope**
Phalaropus lobatus

| S | S | A | W | COAST, FRESH, MARSH

Rare summer visitor to N Isles; elsewhere scarce passage migrant to coasts and inland pools. **ID** Smaller and daintier than Grey Phalarope with very fine, all black bill. Unmistakable in breeding plumage. Often very tame and feeds by pecking rapidly from side to side while spinning on surface of water. During breeding season female more brightly coloured than male. **NEST** In poolside tussock.

male breeding

★★ Nightjar *Caprimulgus europaeus*

| s | S | A | W | COAST, HEATH, MOOR, WOOD

Fairly common but localised summer visitor. **ID** A characteristic bird of heathland, moorland and clear-fell areas of woodland; crepuscular habits and excellent camouflage make it very difficult to observe well. Female lacks white spots near wing tips and on corners of tail. Falcon-like flight silhouette with long, pointed wings and long, narrow tail. Flies silently except when wing-clapping in courtship display or calling. **VOICE** Unforgettable churring that can continue seemingly for hours at a time from dusk until dawn, especially on calm, balmy nights. Flight call a distinctive 'too-ik'. **NEST** Simple hollow on ground, often near to piece of old wood.

male

★ Cuckoo *Cuculus canorus*

| S | S | A | W | FARM, HEATH, PARK, REEDS, WOOD

Common summer visitor. **ID** Slim with pointed wings and long, rounded tail, giving impression of a small falcon or Sparrowhawk. Some females grey on head, breast and upperparts, as are males. Wings often held drooped at rest, and in flight do not rise above the horizontal. **VOICE** Male gives the familiar 'cuckoo', female a bubbling trill. **NEST** Eggs laid in other birds' nests, parasitising particularly Dunnock, Meadow Pipit and Reed Warbler, the species chosen to match that in which the female Cuckook herself was reared.

female

★ Turtle Dove *Streptopelia turtur*

| S | S | A | W | FARM, SCRUB, WOOD

Common but declining summer visitor to England and Wales. **ID** Smallest and slimmest of our doves. Bright orange on closed wing; striped black and white neck patch; broad white tip to tail conspicuous in flight. Often seen in pairs. **VOICE** Gentle purring. **NEST** In bush, hedgerow or small tree.

★ Collared Dove
Streptopelia decaocto <

| S | S | A | W | BUILDINGS, FARM, GARDEN, PARK

Very common resident. **ID** A social bird, usually found in pairs or groups. Colour of the night-time drink Horlicks. Deep crimson iris. In flight, tail feathers broadly tipped white. Often chased in flight by House Sparrows. **VOICE** Song a repetitive and monotonous trisyllabic 'you-nigh-ted', with the middle syllable drawn out and stressed. Also a harsh 'cree-arr' on landing or while being chased in flight. **NEST** In a tree, often an evergreen.

★★ Waxwing *Bombycilla garrulus* >

| S | S | A | W | FARM, GARDEN

Scarce to fairly common but unpredictable winter visitor from N and E Europe. **ID** Rotund Starling-sized bird with a thick crest. Bright yellow tips to flight feathers and tail, and sealing-wax-red tips to secondaries larger and brighter in males. Gregarious and approachable but always remains wary while feeding on berries or fruit, e.g. cotoneaster, rowan and pyracantha. **VOICE** Distinctive ringing trill, likened to a small bell; once heard never forgotten.

male

★★ Dipper *Cinclus cinclus*

| S | S | A | W | FRESH, MOOR, MOUNTAIN

Localised resident. **ID** A dumpy, Wren-shaped bird with a short tail usually seen bobbing on rocks in the middle of fast-flowing streams. White eyelid visible as it blinks. Our only passerine that swims, which it does both on the surface and underwater. Low, direct flight over water. **VOICE** A sharp, metallic 'zinc'. **NEST** Domed with a side entrance, on ledge, in cavity on bridge or amongst tree roots, overlooking and often overhanging water.

★ Mistle Thrush *Turdus viscivorus*

| S | S | A | W | FARM, GARDEN, HEATH, PARK, WOOD

Very common resident and partial migrant. **ID** Our largest thrush; more upright stance than Song Thrush with boldly marked, rounded spots on underparts. In flight, longish tail, white 'armpits' and underwing; purposeful bounding flight. **VOICE** A loud, far-carrying song consisting of a simple, short, oft-repeated phrase given from the top of a tree; has a melancholy quality. Sings from late December onwards, often in windy or wet weather, hence the vernacular name of 'Storm Cock'. Churring call given in flight or when alarmed. **NEST** In fork of tree or shrub, often at a considerable height.

★ Fieldfare *Turdus pilaris*

| S | S | A | W | FARM, MOOR, PARK, WOOD

Rare breeder and abundant winter visitor from N Europe. **ID** Appears larger than Blackbird, having longer wings and tail. In flight pale grey rump and white underwing (like Mistle Thrush). Gregarious and often associates with Redwings and Starlings. Dive-bombs and defecates on intruders in breeding territory. **VOICE** Flight calls a chattering 'tchak, tchak, tchak' and a quieter 'see'. Song a brief simple chattering. **NEST** In fork of tree, usually in loose colony.

★ Song Thrush *Turdus philomelos*

| S | S | A | W | FARM, GARDEN, PARK, WOOD

Abundant resident and partial migrant, common autumn passage migrant and winter visitor from Europe. **ID** A familiar garden bird but has declined in recent years. Heavily spotted underparts; lack of 'eyebrow' and buff flanks separate it from Redwing. In flight, buff 'armpits' and underwing. Breaks open snail shells on stones, known as 'a thrush's anvil'. **VOICE** A loud song that may continue for several minutes in which each phrase is repeated 2–3 times. Alarm call a single 'tchik', softer than that of a Robin; flight call a soft 'sip', lacking the buzzing quality of a Redwing. **NEST** In tree or shrub, often close to the trunk.

★ **Redwing** *Turdus iliacus*

| S | S | **A** | **W** | FARM, GARDEN, PARK, WOOD

Rare breeder in Scotland; very common winter visitor from Fennoscandia and Iceland. **ID** Like Song Thrush but white or creamy 'eyebrow', chestnut flanks and streaked not spotted breast. In flight, chestnut 'armpits' and underwing. Often in mixed flock with Fieldfares. **VOICE** A thin 'tseep' in flight, often heard at night on migration, especially in October. **NEST** In tree or shrub.

★ **Blackbird** *Turdus merula*

| **S** | **S** | **A** | **W** | FARM, GARDEN, PARK, WOOD

Abundant resident, common winter visitor and passage migrant, mainly in autumn from N Europe. **ID** One of our most familiar birds. Male is black with a yellow bill and eye ring. **VOICE** Song a fairly short, loud, melodious warbling, the whole song being repeated at frequent intervals. Clucks when alarmed and gives a distinctive chattering call in flight. **NEST** In low tree, shrub or hedgerow.

female

★ **Chiffchaff** *Phylloscopus collybita* <

`S S A W` FARM, WOOD

Very common summer visitor; scarce winter visitor but becoming more numerous. **ID** Very similar to Willow Warbler, but appears shorter and less sleek. Very short winged with tip of closed wing barely reaching base of tail; browner above and buffer below than Willow Warbler; dark legs Restless and frequently flicks tail down. **VOICE** Call 'hoceet' with rising inflection at end. Song the familiar 'chiff, chaff, chiff, chaff, chiff, chiff, chaff...'. **NEST** Domed structure just above ground level in vegetation or shrub.

★ **Reed Warbler** *Acrocephalus scirpaceus*

`S S A W` FRESH, REEDS, SCRUB

Common summer visitor. **ID** The common warbler of extensive reedbeds. A sleek-looking bird with a flat forehead and long, thin bill; inconspicuous short, pale 'eyebrow' in front of eye; unstreaked both above and below. **VOICE** Song a rather boring chatter with little variation in pitch or notes, each phrase repeated 2–3 times, given from deep in the reeds or from the top of a stem. Alarm call a low churring. **NEST** Usually in reedbed colony. Nest built around several reed stems growing in the water.

★★★ **Marsh Warbler** *Acrocephalus palustris*

`S S A W` FARM, FRESH, SCRUB

Rare summer visitor and passage migrant from W Europe. **ID** Very similar to Reed Warbler and in field best told by song. Less sleek appearance than Reed Warbler with a more rounded crown and shorter bill producing a subtly different profile; generally a colder grey, more olive plumage lacking the warm rufous brown of Reed Warbler; legs yellowish-pink. **VOICE** Sings for long, unbroken periods, often from dense cover; song an amazing mix of various calls and songs of other species encountered in both its summer and winter quarters; undoubtedly Europe's best avian mimic. **NEST** A metre or more up in tall vegetation or shrub.

★ **Garden Warbler** *Sylvia borin*

| S | S | A | W | GARDEN, SCRUB, WOOD

Very common summer visitor. **ID** Few
distinguishing features. Size of more familiar
Blackcap; indistinct pale eye ring; unstreaked above
and below; legs bluish-grey. **VOICE** Song similar to
Blackcap but more mellow and more sustained.
Often sings from deep inside cover, making
songster difficult to locate. Alarm call a rather soft
'tcheck'. **NEST** In low shrub or sapling.

★★ **Cetti's Warbler** *Cettia cetti*

| S | S | A | W | FRESH, REEDS, SCRUB

Scarce but increasing resident of lowland river
valleys. **ID** Far more often heard than seen. Rather
plump, short-necked warbler with broad, rounded
tail, often held partly raised; short, whitish 'eyebrow';
white eye ring around lower lid. Skulks low down in
undergrowth like a mouse. **VOICE** Sudden, short,
explosive song, incorporating 'cetti, cetti'. **NEST** Low
down in thick herbage.

★ **Nightingale**
Luscinia megarhynchos

| S | S | A | W | HEATH, SCRUB, WOOD

Fairly common but declining summer visitor. **ID** An
elusive bird that is far more often heard than seen.
Featureless, except for bright chestnut rump and
tail; pale eye ring in otherwise plain face. **VOICE** Its
famous song is loud and musical, with each
rounded, full-bodied note being repeated several
times; may sing continuously for several minutes.
Characteristic notes include a liquid 'wheet',
bubbling 'chook-chook-chook' and 'pew-pew-pew'
rising in a crescendo. **NEST** Well concealed on or
near ground under shrubs.

female

★ **Blackcap** *Sylvia atricapilla*

| S | S | A | W | FARM, GARDEN, WOOD

Very common summer visitor and scarce winter visitor from Central Europe. **ID** Female greyish-brown above and paler below, with chestnut cap; lacks white in tail. Male greyer above with a black cap. **VOICE** Call a hard 'tac, tac', louder than Lesser Whitethroat. Song a rich, fluty warble, more varied but less sustained than Garden Warbler. **NEST** Above ground in low bush, brambles, evergreen or other woody vegetation.

★ **Lesser Whitethroat** *Sylvia curruca*

| S | S | A | W | FARM, PARK, SCRUB

Common summer visitor and fairly common passage migrant. **ID** Smaller and more skulking than Whitethroat, with greyish-brown upperparts, dark cheek and dark grey legs. **VOICE** Call a single 'tick'. Song a preliminary subdued, brief warble followed by a boring rattle on a single note. **NEST** Low down in a bush or conifer.

★ **Whitethroat** *Sylvia communis*

| S | S | A | W | FARM, HEATH, SCRUB

Very common summer visitor. **ID** As name implies, has distinct white throat; broad chestnut area on closed wing; straw-coloured legs; tail often cocked. Male has grey head and pinkish underparts. A restless bird, darting in and out of cover. **VOICE** Hoarse, scolding 'tchair'. Song an oft-repeated brief, scratchy chattering, given during dancing song flight or from top of bush. **NEST** In low shrub or tall plants, e.g. nettles, about 30cm off ground.

female

male

★★ **Pied Flycatcher** *Ficedula hypoleuca*

| S | S | A | W | COAST, WOOD

Localised summer visitor; fairly common autumn passage migrant from Scandinavia. **ID** Both sexes have white wing flashes and white sides to tail. Male is black above and white below. A very active small flycatcher that is rarely still; even when perched it has the habit of flicking its tail and one wing. **VOICE** Call a frequently repeated 'whit' or anxious 'phweet'. An uninspiring song consisting of a repetition of two notes with an occasional trill. **NEST** In hole in tree or in a nest box.

female

★★★ **Red-breasted Flycatcher**
Ficedula parva

| S | S | A | W | SCRUB, WOOD

Rare visitor from NE Europe to coastal areas. **ID** Our smallest flycatcher. Narrow white eye ring; broad white base to dark tail feathers, especially noticeable as bird flies away. Male has reddish-orange throat and upper breast. Very restless, constantly on move, feeding warbler-like in canopy, but occasionally sits still on perch, when it flicks tail and droops wings. **VOICE** Quiet Wren-like chatter and sharp 'chik'.

male

female

★ **Spotted Flycatcher** *Muscicapa striata*

| S | S | A | W | BUILDINGS, FRESH, GARDEN, PARK, WOOD

Common, but declining, summer visitor. **ID** Characteristic upright stance as it sits on an exposed perch awaiting passing insect prey. Grey-brown streaks on breast and crown, rather than spots as name implies; dark, broad-based bill; short black legs. Sits on perch, flicking its tail, before sallying out to catch insects in flight, then returning. **VOICE** Not particularly vocal. Short, simple song a mixture of odd notes and trills. Contact call a short 'tzee'; when alarmed a sharp 'tzee, tick, tick'. **NEST** In hollow in tree trunk, small fork in tree or amongst creepers on trunk or wall of building.

★ **Sand Martin** *Riparia riparia*

| S | S | A | W | COAST, FRESH, REEDS

Very common but localised summer visitor. **ID** Smaller and shorter-winged than Swallow, with no tail streamers. Plain brown upperparts and well-defined brown breast band on white underparts. Highly gregarious; feeds mainly over fresh water. **VOICE** A chirruping call heard most often around colonies when alarmed or excited. **NEST** In colonies, individual burrows tunnelled into a vertical bank of sand or soft soil.

★★★ **Water Pipit** *Anthus spinoletta*

| S | S | A | W | COAST, FRESH, MARSH

Rare winter visitor from S Europe. **ID** In breeding plumage has grey head and pinkish tinge to breast, when can be confused with Scandinavian race of Rock Pipit (*A.p.littoralis*). In winter very similar to Rock Pipit but paler underparts, whiter 'eyebrow', white wing bars and white outer tail feathers. Unlike Rock Pipit, favours inland wetland sites, especially watercress beds. **VOICE** Flight call a single, thin 'tseep', compared with short run of notes given by Meadow Pipit.

breeding

★ **Marsh Tit** *Poecile palustris*

| S | S | A | W | GARDEN, PARK, WOOD

Common but declining resident. **ID** Very similar to Willow Tit and often best separated by voice, but Marsh Tit has glossy black cap, small neat black bib, paler underparts and lacks a pale panel on closed wing; viewed from below tail appears square ended. Often found in pairs, even in winter. **VOICE** Call an explosive 'pitchoo' and nasal 'tchair'. Song a fairly loud and repetitive 'tchupp, tchupp, tchupp...'. **NEST** In hole in tree or stump.

★★ **Willow Tit** *Poecile montana*

| s | s | a | w | WOOD

Fairly common but declining resident. **ID** Very similar to Marsh Tit; best to confirm identification by voice. Willow Tit has dull black cap, more extensive bib that is wider at lower border than at base of bill, buffer flanks and pale edges to secondaries on closed wing; viewed from below tail appears more rounded due to shorter outer tail feathers. Despite their names, Willow Tits tend to be found in damper areas of woodland than Marsh Tits. **VOICE** Call easily recognised once learnt: 'tzi, tzi, chaar, chaar, chaar', the last three notes rather drawn out and hoarse. Song 'tu, tu, tu, tu...', recalling Nightingale or Wood Warbler. **NEST** Excavates its own nesting cavity in rotten tree stump.

★ **Coal Tit** *Periparus ater*

| s | s | a | w | GARDEN, WOOD

Very common resident. **ID** A typical bird of coniferous woodland, its thin bill allowing it to feed between pine needles. White patch on nape; broad black bib. **VOICE** Call 'tsui' with rising inflection at end and other thin calls very like those of Goldcrest. Song an oft-repeated 'peechoo'. **NEST** In hole, low down, on ground, in bank, in rock crevice or amongst tree roots.

★★ **Crested Tit** *Lophophanes cristatus*

| s | s | a | w | WOOD

Scarce resident in Scotland. **ID** A characteristic bird of Caledonian pine forests, not always easy to locate but unmistakable if seen well. Black and white head topped by a speckled, pointed crest. **VOICE** Call a bubbling, purring trill, not unlike Long-tailed Tit but deeper. Song a rapid series of high-pitched 'tzee, tzee, tzee'. **NEST** Excavates own hole in rotten tree trunk or stump.

★★ **Hawfinch** *Coccothraustes coccothraustes* >

| S | S | A | W | PARK, WOOD

Fairly common but localised resident. **ID** Large finch with very powerful, heavy bill. Strange club-shaped extensions on inner primaries. In flight, prominent white tip to tail and white wing bar. Often found in vicinity of hornbeams. Very wary and despite flocking in winter can be extremely elusive. **VOICE** A Robin-like 'tzic'. **NEST** On horizontal branch of tree at varying height, often in loose colony of a few pairs.

★ **Chaffinch** *Fringilla coelebs*

| S | S | A | W | FARM, GARDEN, HEATH, PARK, WOOD

Abundant resident and winter visitor, mainly from Scandinavia **ID** One of our most widespread birds and the second commonest. Male has blue head and pinkish-chestnut underparts. In winter sexes often found in separate flocks. **VOICE** Cheerful 'spink' and a difficult to locate 'hcoeet'. Song a vigorous cascade with a terminal flourish, tirelessly repeated after a short interval and often fo lowed by a nearby rival's song. **NEST** In fork of tree or bush.

female

★ **Goldfinch** *Carduelis carduelis*

| S | S | A | W | FARM, GARDEN, PARK, SCRUB, WOOD

Very common and increasing resident and partial migrant. **ID** Unusually pointed bill for a finch. Sexes very similar with bright yellow wing bars in flight; male has more extensive red on face. Feeds on thistles and teasels. **VOICE** Cheerful, trisyllabic flight call, 'swit, wit, wit'. Song a mixture of rapid trills and twitters, incorporating the flight call. **NEST** In crown of tree, often on thinner, outer branch.

male

★ Linnet *Carduelis cannabina*

| S | S | A | W | FARM, HEATH, SCRUB

Very common resident and partial migrant. **ID** Brown upperparts, warmer chestnut in male; primaries edged white, creating a diffuse, ill-defined pale wing panel in flight. Female streaky brown, lacking pink on breast. Flocks in winter and spring. **VOICE** Flight call a rapid twittering. Song a rather quiet, musical twittering delivered from the top of a bush. **NEST** In thick bush, often gorse, and frequently in loose colony.

★ Greenfinch *Carduelis chloris*

| S | S | **A** | **W** | FARM, GARDEN, PARK, SCRUB, WOOD

Very common resident; fairly common winter visitor from N Europe, mainly Norway. **ID** A bulky finch with a fairly heavy, triangular bill; yellow in wings and tail. Male is more brightly coloured. Butterfly-like display flight with male flying in circles while singing. **VOICE** Flight call a soft 'chup', also gives a buzzing 'dzweee' while perched. Song a Canary-like trill mixed with twittering. **NEST** In fork of tree or bush.

female

female

★★ Brambling *Fringilla montifringilla*

| S | S | **A** | W | FARM, GARDEN, WOOD

Occasional breeder in Scotland; common winter visitor, mainly from Fennoscandia. **ID** Size and shape of Chaffinch; orange tinge to breast in all plumages with dark, round spots on flanks; rump white. Male has blacker head and is generally brighter, especially in breeding plumage. Associates with Chaffinches and is often found feeding on beech mast in winter. **VOICE** Loud, harsh, questioning 'tchweep' and quiet 'tchup'.

★ **Robin** *Erithacus rubecula*

| S | S | A | W | FARM, GARDEN, WOOD

Abundant resident; fairly common passage migrant from
N Europe mainly in autumn. **ID** One of our most familiar
birds, aided by its appearance on Christmas cards.
VOICE A short, sharp 'tic'. Song consists of a collection of
rather thin notes, varying in volume and speed. One of the
few birds to sing throughout the winter; on occasion also
sings at night by the light of a street lamp, when it may be
mistaken for a Nightingale. **NEST** Well concealed in hollow
on bank, or in cavity in tree stump, wall or thick scrub.

female

★★★ **Bluethroat** *Luscinia svecica*

| S | S | A | W | SCRUB

Rare visitor from continental Europe to coastal areas. **ID**
Whitish 'eyebrow'; chestnut at base of tail, especially
visible in flight. Only adult male has significant area of
blue on throat. Actions much as Robin; flicks tail when
perched. Two races: Red-spotted (*L.s.svecica*) from N
Europe and White-spotted (*L.s.cyanecula*) from S and
Central Europe. **VOICE** A sharp 'tac'.

★ **Redstart** *Phoenicurus phoenicurus*

| S | S | A | W | PARK, SCRUB, WOOD

Common summer visitor; fairly common passage migrant
from Scandinavia, mainly in autumn. **ID** Slim and upright
stance. In spring male is blue-grey above and bright
chestnut below. Chestnut tail constantly quivered.
Rarely seen on ground. **VOICE** Call an anxious 'wee-tik-tik'
and thin 'wheet'. Short song, sweet, if slightly hoarse, rather
like a Robin's with a terminal twitter. **NEST** In hole, generally
in tree, but occasionally in wall or shed.

female

female

★ **Wheatear** *Oenanthe oenanthe*

| S | S | A | W | COAST, FARM, HEATH, MOOR, MOUNTAIN

Common summer visitor and fairly common passage migrant from Iceland and Greenland. **ID** Readily identified on ground by upright stance and white rump, especially visible as bird flies away. Male in breeding plumage has blue-grey back and black mask through eye. Restless, constantly on move, bobbing or fanning tail. Greenland and Iceland race (*O.o.leucorhoa*) larger, more boldly marked and with a tendency to perch on bushes. **VOICE** Call a hard 'check', although often silent on migration. Song brief, explosive and rapid. **NEST** In hole in rocky crevice, stone wall or rabbit burrow.

★★★ **Red-backed Shrike**
Lanius collurio

| S | S | A | W | HEATH, SCRUB

Rare summer visitor and passage migrant from N Europe. **ID** Perches in open but can be surprisingly elusive. Male has blue-grey head and black mask through eye. When perched often swings tail from side to side; tail appears fairly long in flight. **VOICE** Harsh, grating 'check'. **NEST** In bush or shrub.

female

female

male

★★ **Bearded Tit** *Panurus biarmicus*

| S | S | A | W | REEDS

Scarce resident and partial migrant. **ID** Lives exclusively in or near reedbeds. Tawny brown bird with a long tail, hence old colloquial name of 'Reed Pheasant'. Male has blue head and black moustache. Whirring flight across tops of reeds, but remains low down in reeds on windy days. **VOICE** Distinctive twanging or pinging calls, given at rest and in flight. **NEST** Low down in reeds, near edge of stand.

★★ **Grasshopper Warbler** *Locustella naevia*

| S | S | A | W | COAST, FRESH, HEATH, MARSH, REEDS, SCRUB

Localised summer visitor. **ID** A skulking, elusive bird more often heard singing than seen. Drab olive-brown with streaked upperparts; rounded tail with dark streaks on undertail coverts. **VOICE** A far-carrying reeling song, varying in volume as head is turned, making it difficult to locate. Song is delivered both day and night. **NEST** Near ground level in a grassy tussock or taller vegetation.

★ **Sedge Warbler** *Acrocephalus schoenobaenus*

| S | S | A | W | FARM, FRESH, MARSH, REEDS, SCRUB

Very common summer visitor. **ID** The common small bird of reedbeds, with a prominent cream 'eyebrow'. **VOICE** Brief song, a mixture of slightly discordant chattering notes interspersed with trills and occasionally including calls or songs of other species. Song given during short ascending and descending flight or from a bush or reed. Alarm calls include a sharp 'tchek' and a churr. **NEST** On ground or low down in tall vegetation or at base of shrub.

★ **Stonechat** *Saxicola torquata*

female

| S | S | A | W | HEATH, MOOR, SCRUB

Common but declining resident and partial migrant. **ID** Plumper and more upright than Whinchat. Male much brighter than female with black head and white half collar in breeding plumage. Often seen on top of bushes and fence posts, when it characteristically jerks wings and tail. **VOICE** Scolding 'wheest, tchack, tchack' like two stones being knocked together. Song rather quiet, short and scratchy, recalling Dunnock. **NEST** On or near ground in vegetation at base of bush.

★ **Whinchat** *Saxicola rubetra*

female

| S | S | A | W | FARM, HEATH, MOOR, SCRUB

Common summer visitor. **ID** Stocky; prominent pale 'eyebrow', white patches at base of tail, which it often flicks. Male has blackish cheeks and white 'eyebrow' in breeding plumage. Flies low over ground. **VOICE** Scolding, sharp 'tic-tic'. Brief, clear, crisp song. **NEST** In tussock on ground, often at base of small bush.

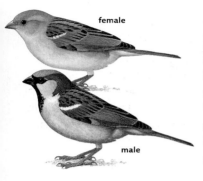

female

male

★ **House Sparrow** *Passer domesticus*

| S | S | A | W | BUILDINGS, FARM, GARDEN

Abundant but declining resident. **ID** Rather dumpy, brown and grey bird with a stout bill. Female lacks distinct head markings and is duller above. **VOICE** Various chirping calls that are strung together as an apology for a song. **NEST** In hole or crevice in a building, or a domed structure in creepers growing up a wall; occasionally in a bush or hedge.

★ **Tree Sparrow** *Passer montanus*

| S | S | A | W | BUILDINGS, COAST, FARM, GARDEN, PARK, WOOD

Common but declining resident. **ID** The country cousin of the familiar House Sparrow. Slightly smaller than House Sparrow with warm chocolate-brown crown and nape contrasting with white face and collar. Neat black bib and black spot on cheek. Sexes similar. Generally noisy, gregarious birds that chatter away to each other. **VOICE** Not dissimilar to House Sparrow, but higher pitched and with a more lively intonation, 'tchick'; flight call a distinctive 'teck, teck'. **NEST** In hole in tree, cliff or building; takes readily to nest boxes.

male
non-breeding

female
breedimg

★★ **Snow Bunting** *Plectrophenax nivalis*

| S | S | A | W | COAST, MOUNTAIN

Rare breeder in Scotland; fairly common winter visitor from Greenland, Iceland and Scandinavia. **ID** Male is black and white in summer, retaining extensive white wing patches in winter. Single birds often tame, but flocks difficult to approach. Feeds in flocks in winter on beaches and coastal fields, resembling drifting snowflakes in flight. **VOICE** Flight call 'prrritt, teu', recalling Little Ringed Plover. Song a brief but musical twitter, often given in flight. **NEST** On ground amongst rocks or boulders.

★ **Skylark** *Alauda arvensis* >

| S | S | A | W | COAST, FARM, HEATH, MOOR

Abundant resident, common passage migrant and winter visitor from NE Europe. **ID** A familiar bird of farmland. Short crest not always visible. In flight, narrow white trailing edge to wing and undulating flight. Usually walks or runs away when approached; often hovers just above ground before landing. **VOICE** Song may last for over ten minutes, a varied mix of notes given from the ground, a perch or in flight, during which songster rises gradually higher into the sky. Flight call a chirrup or rolling 'prreet'. **NEST** On ground, often concealed by low vegetation.

★★ **Woodlark** *Lullula arborea*

| S | S | A | W | FARM, HEATH, WOOD

Fairly common but localised resident and partial migrant. **ID** Smaller than Skylark with shorter tail. Broad white 'eyebrows' join on nape; black and white bars at bend of closed wing. In flight, short, triangular wings with a noticeably short, white-tipped tail. When approached tends to run away, only taking flight at last minute. **VOICE** Song given from perch or in flight during which bird soars in wide circles before dropping to ground; a beautiful cascade interspersed with rich trills, 'lu-lu-lu-lu'. Flight call a melodious, trisyllabic 'too-loo-ee'. **NEST** On disturbed ground, usually sheltered by low vegetation.

★ **Meadow Pipit** *Anthus pratensis*

| S | S | A | W | COAST, FARM, HEATH, MOOR, MOUNTAIN

Abundant resident and partial migrant, very common passage migrant and winter visitor from N Europe. **ID** Our commonest pipit, a characteristic bird of open areas such as meadows, heaths and uplands. Upperparts heavily streaked; white eye ring. **VOICE** Song a repetitive series of 'tsi, tsi, tsi' notes with a terminal flourish, given as the bird rises into air then parachutes back to ground. Flight call a run of 2–3 thin notes: 'tseep, tseep, tseep'. **NEST** On ground, often well concealed amongst low vegetation.

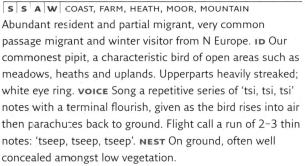

★ Tree Pipit *Anthus trivialis*

| S | S | A | W | HEATH, PARK, SCRUB, WOOD

Common but declining summer visitor. **ID** Very similar to Meadow Pipit but appears slightly longer and plumper; whitish 'eyebrow', bolder streaking on breast where spots tend to coalesce. In woodland, inhabits more open scrubby areas and forest clearings. **VOICE** Song a cascading series of notes with a terminal trill, given in song flight as it parachutes down to a perch. Flight call 'tzee', sharper than that of Meadow Pipit. **NEST** On ground amongst low vegetation.

★ Rock Pipit *Anthus petrosus*

| S | S | A | W | COAST

Common but localised resident and winter visitor from N Europe. **ID** A characteristic passerine of rocky coasts. Larger, heavier and darker than Meadow Pipit; pale grey outer tail feathers; dark legs. **VOICE** Song like Meadow Pipit but no terminal flourish; given during parachuting song flight. Flight call an explosive single 'tzeep'. **NEST** On ground in shallow hole in bank or rocky crevice.

★★★ Water Pipit *Anthus spinoletta*

non-breeding

| S | S | A | W | COAST, FRESH, MARSH

Rare winter visitor from S Europe. **ID** In winter very similar to Rock Pipit but paler underparts, whiter 'eyebrow', white wing bars and white outer tail feathers. Unlike Rock Pipit, favours inland wetland sites, especially watercress beds. **VOICE** Flight call a single, thin 'tseep', compared with short run of notes given by Meadow Pipit.

★★ Shorelark *Eremophila alpestris*

male breeding

| S | S | A | W | COAST, FARM, MOUNTAIN

Scarce autumn passage migrant and winter visitor from N Europe; has bred on Scottish mountain tops. **ID** Distinct black and yellow head pattern at all seasons. Female duller than male. Also known as the Horned Lark due to short black 'horns'. **VOICE** Flight call like that of Meadow Pipit, a short single or double 'psee, psee'. **NEST** In hollow on ground, often by stone or tuft of vegetation.

female

★ **Reed Bunting** *Emberiza schoeniclus*

S S A W FARM, FRESH, REEDS, SCRUB

Very common resident and partial migrant. **ID** One of the most familiar birds of reedbeds and reed-fringed pools due to the male's habit of singing from a prominent perch. A heavily streaked bird with buffish 'eyebrow', small dark bill, white sides to tail; our only bunting with chestnut lesser coverts. **VOICE** Call a distinctive 'sieoo' with a downward inflection. Song, which starts slowly but speeds up, is a short, discordant collection of notes: 'tseek, tseek, tseek, tississik'. **NEST** On ground in grassy tussock or clump of rushes, or in a low bush.

★★ **Lapland Bunting** *Calcarius lapponicus*

S S **A W** COAST, FARM

Scarce winter visitor and passage migrant from Fennoscandia. **ID** Stockier than Reed Bunting with a paler cheek, a pale yellow bill and a chestnut mid-wing panel outlined with white borders. Male in breeding plumage has extensive area of black on head and breast. Usually very wary, running along ground to escape detection rather than taking flight. Often feeds in fields in company with Skylarks. **VOICE** Flight call a short rattle followed by a plaintive note: 'ticky, tick, tioo'. Can sound very similar to Snow Bunting.

female

★ **Corn Bunting** *Emberiza calandra*

S S **A W** FARM

Common but declining resident. **ID** A large, dumpy, streaked but otherwise featureless bunting. Stout, yellowish bill; no white in tail. May fly with legs dangling. Polygamous; gregarious outside breeding season. **VOICE** Flight call a short sharp 'bit'. Song a discordant, accelerating jangle, like a bunch of keys being rattled. **NEST** On ground amongst vegetation, or in low hedge.

female

★ **Yellowhammer** *Emberiza citrinella*

| S | S | A | W | FARM, HEATH, SCRUB

Abundant but declining resident. **ID** Chestnut rump and conspicuous white outer tail feathers visible on flying away. Male has bright yellow head and underparts. Often perches conspicuously on top of bush, tree or wires. **VOICE** Flight call a single, metallic 'chip' or double 'pit, pit'. Song the familiar 'a little bit of bread and no cheeeese'. **NEST** Well concealed in grass or vegetation at base of hedge or on side of overgrown bank.

★★ **Cirl Bunting** *Emberiza cirlus*

| S | S | A | W | FARM

female

Scarce and localised resident. **ID** Female very similar to female Yellowhammer, but with olive-grey rump and suggestion of male's darker face markings. Male has black eye stripe and throat, and olive-green breast band. **VOICE** Call a sharp 'sip'. Song recalls Lesser Whitethroat, being a short but continuous rattle on a single note. **NEST** Low down in hedge or thick bush.

★ **Dunnock** *Prunella modularis*

| S | S | A | W | FARM, GARDEN, SCRUB, WOOD

Abundant resident and fairly common passage migrant from N Europe. **ID** A sparrow-like bird but with a thin, warbler-like bill. Blue-grey around head and upper breast. Shuffles around flicking its wings, rarely far from cover. A nervous bird, afraid of its own shadow! **VOICE** Call a thin, squeaky 'tew'. Song a fairly brief, weak jingle, often given from the top of a bush. **NEST** In bush, hedge, evergreen or other area of cover.

★★ **Twite** *Carduelis flavirostris*

| S | S | A | W | COAST, HEATH, MOOR, MOUNTAIN

Localised resident and partial migrant. **ID** Very similar to female Linnet with few distinguishing features, but more streaky and warmer buff with less white in wing; yellow bill in winter. Male in breeding plumage has pink rump. Forms dense winter flocks. **VOICE** Call a diagnostic nasal 'tzweet' included in constant twittering given in flight. Song fast trills and buzzing notes. **NEST** On open ground amongst low cover.

non-breeding

female

★ **Linnet** *Carduelis cannabina*

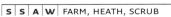

| S | S | A | W | FARM, HEATH, SCRUB

Very common resident and partial migrant. **ID** Brown head and upperparts, warmer chestnut in male; primaries edged white. Male in breeding plumage has red on forehead and breast. Flocks in winter and spring. **VOICE** Flight call a rapid twittering. Song a rather quiet, musical twittering delivered from the top of a bush. **NEST** In thick bush, often gorse, and frequently in loose colony.

★ **Lesser Redpoll** *Carduelis cabaret*

| S | S | A | W | HEATH, WOOD

Common but declining resident and partial migrant. **ID** Small, heavily streaked finch with red forehead, black bib and pale wing bars. Male in breeding plumage has pink breast. Usually seen in tops of birches or alders, in winter not infrequently in mixed flocks with Siskins. Female Common (Mealy) Redpoll (*Carduelis flammea*), a winter visitor from N Fennoscandia, is slightly larger than Lesser Redpoll, generally paler and greyer with white wing bars and a whitish, streaked rump. **VOICE** Rapid, high-pitched, metallic trill in flight. Song similar to flight calls, given from top of birch or in song flight. **NEST** Often high in tree or tall bush, usually in loose colony.

female

male

★ **Wren** *Troglodytes troglodytes*

| S | S | A | W | FARM, GARDEN, HEATH, PARK, SCRUB, WOOD

Abundant resident and partial migrant. **ID** A popular and well-known bird due to its small size, plump shape and short, often cocked-up tail. Always active, rarely still. Very inquisitive and can easily be attracted by making squeaking noises. Rapid whirring flight. **VOICE** Song easily recognised by its loud, explosive quality. Alarm calls include a harsh 'chit' and a distinctive churring. **NEST** Domed structure built into a natural or artificial cavity.

★★ **Wryneck** *Jynx torquilla*

| S | S | A | W | COAST, PARK, SCRUB, WOOD

Rare breeding summer visitor and passage migrant from W Europe. **ID** Vermiculated grey and brown upperparts with a black line along back; longish, rounded, barred tail. Crown feathers erected if alarmed; able to turn head almost 360 degrees. Feeds on ground on ants and can be surprisingly elusive. **VOICE** Alarm call a series of 'kee, kee, kee' notes. **NEST** In hole or cavity in tree, wall or building.

★ **Treecreeper** *Certhia familiaris*

| S | S | A | W | FARM, PARK, WOOD

Very common resident. **ID** A small, well-camouflaged bird, appearing like a mouse as it jerkily climbs up a tree trunk. Long, thin, slightly decurved bill for probing crevices in bark. Climbs up trees in spiral fashion, never climbing downwards. In winter, often associates with mixed flocks of foraging tits and Goldcrests. **VOICE** Thin, high-pitched song not unlike a Goldcrest but with a terminal descending trill. **NEST** In narrow cavity behind loose bark on tree.

★★★ **White-tailed Eagle**
Haliaeetus albicilla   >

| S | S | A | W | COAST

Rare Scottish resident and winter visitor from N Europe. **ID** Very large eagle with broad, parallel-sided wings, large head with massive bill and shortish, wedge-shaped white tail. Shallow, relaxed wing beats with only the occasional glide. Catches fish with talons from surface of water. **NEST** In tree top or on cliff face or rocky pinnacle.

★★★ **Golden Eagle**
Aquila chrysaetos   >

| S | S | A | W | MOUNTAIN

Rare and localised resident in N. **ID** Very large, with long wings and long tail. Dark brown plumage with golden tinge around nape; greyish flight feathers. Deep, powerful wing beats with frequent glides, when wings held in shallow V. **NEST** Usually on rocky ledge, occasionally in tree.

★★ **Red Kite** *Milvus milvus*

| S | S | A | W | FARM, MOOR, PARK, WOOD

Scarce but increasing resident, aided by recent re-introduction programmes; rare spring migrant from Europe. **ID** Large, long-winged raptor with long, deeply forked chestnut tail. In flight, very pale, almost white primaries from below. Effortless, buoyant flight with wings arched and swept backwards from mid-wing; uses tail as rudder. **VOICE** Buzzard-like mewing. **NEST** At variable height in tree.

★ **Common Buzzard** *Buteo buteo*

| S | S | A | W | FARM, MOOR, MOUNTAIN, WOOD

Common resident. **ID** Broad wings with 'fingered' tips and short tail, fanned when soaring. Plumage very variable, but in flight from below generally dark body and wing coverts contrasting with paler flight feathers; tail pale with about six narrow, dark bars. Often perches on telegraph poles and fence posts. Soars for long periods, often in small groups, with wings held in shallow V; occasionally hovers. **VOICE** More vocal than other raptors, commonest flight call a loud, plaintive mewing. **NEST** In tree or on rocky ledge.

★★★ **Honey Buzzard** *Pernis apivorus*

| S | S | A | W | WOOD

Rare summer visitor and passage migrant, mainly in autumn. **ID** Longer wings and tail than Common Buzzard, with small cuckoo-like head and slim neck. Very variable underparts from pale to uniformly dark brown body and underwing coverts. Male has grey head and broad dark tip to tail with two narrower bars near base. Female has more barred underwings and more evenly spaced dark bars on tail. Has flatter, more elastic wings in flight than Common Buzzard, and does not hover. In breeding season heavily dependent on diet of adult and larval wasps and bees. **NEST** High in a tree, usually on an old crow's nest.

★★★ **Rough-legged Buzzard** *Buteo lagopus*

| S | S | A | W | FARM, HEATH, PARK

Rare winter visitor from Scandinavia. **ID** Larger and longer winged than Common Buzzard. Underparts very pale with dark belly and white tail with broad, dark terminal band. Distinct black mid-wing patches also visible from below in flight. Frequently hovers on slowly beating wings.

★★★ Osprey
Pandion haliaetus

| S | S | A | W | COAST, FRESH

Rare summer visitor. **ID** Long, narrow wings; dark above and pale below with darker band across breast. Distinctive flight silhouette with angled wings and the bend in the wing held forwards while gliding. Hovers over water before diving and taking fish from water with talons. **NEST** On tree top or rocky outcrop.

★★ Marsh Harrier
Circus aeruginosus

| S | S | A | W | FARM, MARSH, REEDS

Scarce but increasing resident and summer visitor. **ID** Narrower wings and longer tail than Common Buzzard, but broader wings than other harriers. Male has contrasting grey, brown and black wings; female has a distinctly pale head and paler leading edge to inner wing. Rather lazy, low, quartering flight; also soars high in air with wings raised in shallow V. **NEST** On platform of dead vegetation in reedbed or on ground amongst cereal or arable crop.

female

★★ Hen Harrier *Circus cyaneus*

| S | S | A | W | COAST, FARM, HEATH, MARSH, MOOR, REED

Scarce breeder, partial migrant and winter visitor from W Europe. **ID** A medium-sized raptor with long wings and tail. Smaller and slimmer winged than Marsh Harrier but larger and broader winged than Montagu's Harrier. Female brown with a white rump, known as 'ring tail'. Male pale grey and black. Low, buoyant flight with wings raised in a shallow V. **NEST** On ground in moorland, usually in shelter of taller vegetation.

female

female

★★★ Montagu's Harrier
Circus pygargus

| S | S | A | W | FARM

Rare summer visitor; one of our rarest breeding birds. **ID** Smaller than Marsh and Hen Harriers, with proportionately longer, narrower wings and long, narrow tail. In flight, female brown with a white rump, known as 'ring tail'. Male pale grey and black. Buoyant, almost tern-like flight, especially in male. **NEST** On ground, nowadays almost invariably amongst crops.

★★ Merlin *Falco columbarius*

| S | S | A | W | COAST, FARM, HEATH, MARSH, MOOR

Fairly common but localised breeder and partial migrant. **ID** The small, dashing falcon of open country that recalls a miniature Peregrine. Indistinct stripe below the eye; broadly barred tail. Male slate grey above. In flight rapid wing beats and occasional glides. **VOICE** Rapid 'ki-ki-ki-ki'. **NEST** Usually on ground in open moorland.

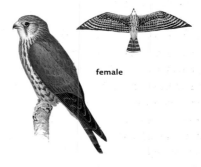

female

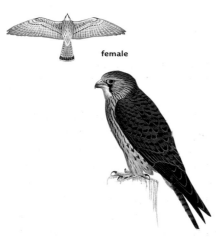

female

★ Kestrel *Falco tinnunculus*

| S | S | A | W | FARM, HEATH, MOOR, PARK, WOOD

Common resident and partial migrant.
ID Generally the most familiar bird of prey, readily identified by its hovering flight. Male has grey-blue head and tail. In flight, long, pointed wings and tail; frequently hovers with tail spread. Often perches on tree or telegraph pole. **VOICE** Shrill 'kee, kee, kee'. **NEST** On ledge or in cavity of a cliff, building or tree.

★ Tawny Owl *Strix aluco* >

| S | S | A | W | FARM, GARDEN, PARK, WOOD

Common resident. **ID** Our commonest woodland owl, but predominantly nocturnal, so more often heard than seen. Plumage may be brownish-grey or greyish-brown; two pale crown stripes and dark iris. Broad, rounded wings in flight. Usually seen by day roosting in tree top, attention often drawn to it through calls of mobbing Blackbirds, Chaffinches, etc. **VOICE** Song a series of hoots; call an explosive 'keewik' with emphasis on the last syllable. **NEST** In hole in tree or rocky crevice, occasionally on ground.

★ Little Owl *Athene noctua* <

| S | S | A | W | BUILDINGS, COAST, FARM, PARK

Fairly common resident in England and Wales. **ID** Our smallest owl, often seen by day. Distinct white 'eyebrows' and yellow iris. Often sits in open in daylight, bobbing when alarmed or excited. Surprisingly rapid, looping flight on short, rounded wings. **VOICE** Song a long drawn-out soft hoot with an upward inflection at end; call a sharp 'kee-wik'. **NEST** In hole in tree, building or rocky crevice.

★ Barn Owl *Tyto alba*

| S | S | A | W | BUILDINGS, COAST, FARM, PARK, SCRUB

Fairly common resident. **ID** The palest of our owls, with a distinctive heart-shaped face. Nocturnal and crepuscular. Rather lazy flight action, but turns suddenly on spotting potential prey, when may hover or drop to ground. The Dark-breasted Barn Owl (*T.a.guttata*) of Central and E Europe is a rare autumn and winter visitor and has darker, golden underparts and greyer upperparts. **VOICE** Distinctive blood-curdling shriek and a shrill squeal. **NEST** In hole in tree, building, rocky crevice or nest box.

★★ Short-eared Owl
Asio flammeus >

| S | S | A | W | FARM, HEATH, MARSH, MOOR

Fairly common but localised resident and winter visitor. **ID** Often seen hunting by day; a large, long-winged owl, paler than a Tawny Owl. Very short ear tufts, barely visible; yellow iris. In flight appears longer winged than Long-eared Owl with narrow white trailing edge to inner wing, b acker wing tips and extensive area of orangey-buff on primaries; breast but not belly streaked darker and fewer, wider bars on tail than Long-eared Owl. Occasionally soars like a Buzzard, but also frequently perches on ground. **VOICE** Very unusual song flight for an owl, often given from fairly high in the sky, accompanied by a series of hoots. **NEST** On ground amongst vegetation.

★★ Long-eared Owl *Asio otus* >

| S | S | A | W | FARM, HEATH, MOOR, SCRUB, WOOD

Fairly common resident and scarce winter visitor. **ID** Slightly smaller and sleeker than Tawny Owl, and rather greyer on upperparts. Long ear tufts erect and visible only when alarmed; orange iris. Appears long-winged in flight, with orange-ish, straw-coloured patch at base of primaries. Compared with Short-eared Owl lacks white trailing edge to inner wing, but belly as well as breast streaked darker and tail is finely barred. Mainly nocturnal but may be seen in flight on migration by day, especially flying in off the sea. **VOICE** Not very vocal but song a series of widely spaced hoots. **NEST** In large, old nest of another species or in a squirrel drey, occasionally on ground.

female

★★ **Black Grouse** *Tetrao tetrix* >

| S | S | A | W | FARM, HEATH, MOOR, WOOD

Localised and declining resident. **ID** Female brown, barred darker, some with notched tail. Males, which are mainly black with lyre-shaped tails, gather into communal display groups, called 'leks', in spring. Male also known as Blackcock and female as Greyhen. **VOICE** Male gives bubbling calls, audible at long range. **NEST** On ground amongst low plants.

★★ **Capercaillie**
Tetrao urogallus >

| S | S | A | W | WOOD

Localised and declining resident in Scotland.
ID Largest grouse in the world, inhabiting Scots pine forests. The mainly black male is 30 per cent larger than the female, which is brown, barred darker, with a rounded, rufous tail. Males gather into 'leks' (display groups) in evening. **VOICE** Dawn song a series of accelerating clicking calls, followed by a 'pop' and a terminal hiss. Male display involves a mixture of guttural, belch-like calls. **NEST** On ground amongst undergrowth, often at base of pine tree.

female

★ **Pheasant** *Phasianus colchicus*

| S | S | A | W | FARM, MARSH, PARK, WOOD

Abundant resident. **ID** Commonest and most familiar game bird. Very long, pointed tail. Female buffy-brown with darker spots. Male much more brightly coloured with green head, red face and rich chestnut body. Runs rapidly to cover rather than taking off, but when it does so is noisy with whirring wings. Polygynous (a male having more than one mate) and often seen in groups. **VOICE** Male gives familiar 'kok, kok'. **NEST** On ground in long grass or amongst tallish vegetation or shrubs.

female

★★ **Golden Pheasant**
Chrysolophus pictus

| S | S | A | W | WOOD |

Scarce and declining introduced resident, mainly found in E Anglia. **ID** Secretive and elusive despite bright colours of male. Very long, pointed tail. Female like Pheasant but proportionately longer tail, dark bars not spots and yellowish legs. Male a vivid mixture of bright red, orange and yellow. **VOICE** Deer-like shriek, higher pitched than Pheasant, recalling quiet or distant Jay. **NEST** On ground in thick cover.

female

★★ **Ptarmigan**
Lagopus mutus

| S | S | A | W | MOUNTAIN |

Fairly common but very localised resident of Scottish mountains. **ID** A typical grouse with white wings and belly at all seasons. In summer, female barred buffy-brown whereas male is grey; in winter both sexes all white except for black tail. **VOICE** A low, harsh, belch-like croak. **NEST** On ground in shelter of rock or patch of vegetation.

female summer

★ Red Grouse *Lagopus lagopus*

male

| S | S | A | W | MOOR, MOUNTAIN

Very common but localised resident. **ID** The resident game bird of moors and mountains. Uniformly warm brown. Female paler than male with paler barring. Rapid flight, whirring wing beats alternating with glides on down-curved wings. **VOICE** On spring nights male call consists of a run of crowing barks ending with a tril . **NEST** On ground amongst heather or rough grass.

male

★ Grey Partridge
Perdix perdix

| S | S | A | W | FARM

Very common but declining resident.
ID Rotund, chicken-like bird with small head and very short neck. Smaller than Red-legged Partridge; both species have reddish tail. Male more brightly marked with larger belly patch. Flies low with whirring wing beats and short, stiff-winged glides. **VOICE** When flushed an excited 'krri, krri, krri'. Song a rather hoarse 'kieerric', with accent on last syllable. **NEST** On ground in tall grass, vegetation or crop.

★ Red-legged Partridge
Alectoris rufa

| S | S | A | W | FARM, HEATH, PARK, SCRUB

Very common resident. **ID** Slightly larger than Grey Partridge and has white face, a necklace of black streaks and bold barring on flanks. In flight, lower back and rump grey compared with brown of Grey Partridge, but tends to run away rather than taking flight. Gregarious, groups of partridges being known as coveys. **VOICE** Distinctive 'chukar', often repeated several times. **NEST** On ground, usually among growing plants and often in shelter of a bush.

★★ **Quail** *Coturnix coturnix*

| S | **S** | A | W | FARM

Scarce summer visitor. **ID** The only migratory game bird in Britain and Ireland, wintering south of the Sahara. Extremely elusive and rarely seen in the open; ventriloquial call adds to difficulty in locating it. Very small for a game bird, resembling a pheasant or partridge chick. Distinctive head markings but rarely seen well enough to appreciate them! Male has blackish throat, female buff throat. Surprisingly long-winged in flight. **VOICE** Trisyllabic 'wet-my-lips', repeated several times. **NEST** On ground, usually among arable crops.

male

★★★ **Corncrake** *Crex crex*

| **S** | **S** | **A** | W | FARM, MARSH

Localised summer visitor to N and W Isles and Ireland. **ID** Far more often heard than seen. A slim bird but with a rounded body. Heavily spotted above, barred on flanks and undertail coverts; chestnut inner wings conspicuous in flight. Crepuscular and very elusive, slipping away on foot rather than taking flight. **VOICE** Rasping, coarse 'crex, crex'. May be imitated by dragging plastic credit card across teeth of a comb. **NEST** Hidden amongst thick ground vegetation or crops.

★★★ **Bittern** *Botaurus stellaris* <

| S | S | A | W | FRESH, REEDS

Rare resident, partial migrant and winter visitor from NW Europe. **ID** Large, all-brown heron, streaked darker. Walks with shoulders hunched; mainly crepuscular in habits. In flight broad wings and trailing feet. **VOICE** Booming of male is far-carrying and recalls the sound of a distant fog horn. It can be reproduced by blowing across the top of an empty glass milk bottle. **NEST** A pile of reeds and sedges in a reedbed.

★★★ **Purple Heron** *Ardea purpurea*

| S | S | A | W | FRESH, MARSH, REEDS

Rare passage migrant from W Europe, mainly in spring. **ID** Slghtly smaller, more slender and darker than Grey Heron, with a more sinuous, serpentine neck, especially visible in flight when it hangs down well below level of body. Longer, narrower bill than Grey Heron, purplish-grey upperparts. In flight, deep curve of neck and legs; large feet extend well beyond tail. **VOICE** Less strident than Grey Heron.

★ **Moorhen** *Gallinula chloropus*

| S | S | A | W | FARM, FRESH, MARSH

Very common lowland resident. **ID** The familiar black water bird of village ponds. Upperparts dark greyish-brown, white undertail coverts, red bill and frontal shield. Moves head back and forth while swimming; flicks tail while walking. **VOICE** Explosive bubbling call and metallic 'kek, kek'. **NEST** Bulky platform of dead vegetation on or by water.

★★ **Water Rail** *Rallus aquaticus*

| S | S | A | W | FRESH, MARSH, REEDS

Fairly common resident and winter visitor. **ID** An elusive bird of the reedbeds that is more often heard than seen. The laterally compressed body is perfectly adapted for slipping between reed stems, as are the long toes for walking on mud or floating vegetation. Weak flight with dangling legs; also swims short distances. **VOICE** A variety of groans and grunts (called 'sharming'), the most common a pig-like squeal, given especially at night. **NEST** On or near ground level in tall vegetation growing in or near water.

★★★ **Spotted Crake** *Porzana porzana*

<

| S | S | A | W | FRESH, MARSH, REEDS

Rare summer visitor and passage migrant, mainly in autumn. **ID** Shape and actions as Water Rail, but short bill, greenish legs and buff undertail coverts; fine white spotting visible only at close range. Some bluish-grey on head and throat. Crepuscular habits. **VOICE** Song a far-carrying whip-like sound, repeated many times. **NEST** On ground, hidden amongst tall vegetation by water.

★★ **Stone Curlew**
Burhinus oedicnemus >

>

| S | S | A | W | FARM, HEATH

Scarce summer visitor. **ID** Large, ungainly wader with a rather hunched appearance, found inland on heaths or farmland. Large yellow eyes an adaptation to its nocturnal habits. Male has more distinct black borders to white bar on wing coverts. In flight, bold black and white wing pattern. Walks or runs rather furtively with body held horizontally, trying to avoid detection. Extremely well camouflaged when standing still or sitting on ground. **VOICE** Loud, penetrating and eerie Curlew-like calls heard mainly at night during breeding season. **NEST** On bare ground.

★★ Jack Snipe *Lymnocryptes minimus* < 🐦

| s | s | A | W | COAST, FRESH, MARSH, REEDS

Fairly common but elusive and localised passage migrant and winter visitor from N Europe. **ID** Noticeably smaller and shorter billed than Snipe. Distinct yellow stripes along back, providing excellent camouflage against fallen reeds. In flight, short, rather rounded wings. Very skulking, preferring to escape detection by remaining motionless, flushing at last moment and then flying only a short distance. Does not 'tower' like Snipe and rarely calls. **VOICE** Occasionally gives a quiet rasping call when flushed.

★ Snipe *Gallinago gallinago* < 🐦

| s | s | A | W | FARM, FRESH, MARSH, MOOR, REEDS

Common but declining resident and winter visitor from N Europe. **ID** One of the most familiar marshland birds, characterised by a long, straight bill. Easily flushed, flying away erratically and often towering. In flight, narrow white trailing edge to upperwings. **VOICE** Song a frequently repeated 'chipper, chipper, chipper...', interspersed with short, rapid dives accompanied by a drumming sound as air vibrates through outer tail feathers; flight call a characteristic rasping squelch. **NEST** On boggy ground, well concealed amongst vegetation.

★ Woodcock *Scolopax rusticola*

| s | s | A | W | FARM, HEATH, SCRUB, WOOD

Common but declining resident and partial migrant; also winter visitor from N Europe. **ID** Very round, dumpy body and long, straight bill. Unlike Snipe, has barred not striped head and strongly barred underparts. In flight, rounded, rather owl-like wings and long bill pointing downwards. Usually seen singly in woodland, as it 'explodes' from ground. **VOICE** Male gives a short series of 'tswick' and belching calls in display flight. **NEST** On ground in open woodland with low cover.

★ **Curlew** *Numenius arquata* >

`S S A W` COAST, FARM, HEATH, MARSH, MOOR

Common but localised breeder and winter visitor to the coast from N Europe. **ID** Our largest wader, with a very long, decurved bill. In flight, white rump extends to lower back; bill is equal to or longer than width of inner wing. Flies in lines or chevrons with slow, rather deliberate wing beats. **VOICE** Call given on taking off and in flight 'courlooeee', with an upward inflection at end. Song a liquid, rhythmic, bubbling trill. **NEST** On ground amongst heather or other low vegetation.

★★ **Whimbrel** *Numenius phaeopus* >

`S S A W` COAST, FARM, MOOR

Scarce summer visitor to Scotland; fairly common passage migrant from N Europe. **ID** Smaller cousin of the Curlew, with a shorter, less decurved bill and darker crown contrasting with pale central crown stripe and 'eyebrow'. In flight, compared with Curlew, bill shorter than width of inner wing and more rapid wing beats. **VOICE** A rapid, tittering trill of seven whistles given in flight. Song a bubbling trill recalling Curlew. **NEST** On ground in the open.

★ **Redshank** *Tringa totanus* <

`S S A W` COAST, FRESH, MARSH, MOOR

Common but declining breeder and winter visitor, mainly from Iceland. **ID** The noisy wader of marshland. Generally grey in winter, with plainer underparts. In flight, shows broad white trailing edge to wing and white rump extending up lower back. Bobs when alarmed. **VOICE** Call when agitated and in flight a loud, ringing 'tleu, leu, leu'. Song given in flight a musical version of the flight call repeated many times. **NEST** On ground in grassy tussock.

non-breeding

non-breeding

★ **Golden Plover** *Pluvialis apricaria*

| S | S | A | W | COAST, FARM, MARSH, MOOR, MOUNTAIN

Common upland breeder; very common lowland winter visitor from Iceland and N Europe. **ID** Smaller and less stout than Grey Plover. Spangled golden upperparts and black present only during breeding season. Rather shy and always alert, favouring drier areas for feeding. In winter gathers into very large flocks, usually on arable land and often mixed with Lapwings. In flight, narrow white wing bar and white underwing. **VOICE** Distinct, plaintive flight call: 'too'. Song a penetrating, rippling trill. **NEST** On ground amongst heather.

★★★ **Dotterel** *Charadrius morinellus*

| S | S | A | W | COAST, FARM, MOUNTAIN

Summer visitor to mountains in N, mainly the Scottish Highlands. **ID** Smaller and squatter than Golden Plover; long pale 'eyebrow' and dark crown. Chestnut lower breast in breeding plumage, when female is more brightly coloured than male. **VOICE** Flight call a soft rolling trill.
NEST Shallow hollow on ground on mountain top.

non-breeding

female

★★ **Ruff** *Philomachus pugnax*

| S | S | A | W | FARM, MARSH

Rare breeder in England; scarce passage migrant and winter visitor from Europe, mainly to coastal marshes in S and E. **ID** Males (Ruffs) considerably larger than females (Reeves). Both sexes show small head on longish neck; medium length, slightly decurved bill; leg colour varies from orangey-red through yellow to greenish; scaly upperparts. In breeding plumage males' ruff and ear tufts vary from rufous or orange to black or white. Often feeds on flooded fields. **NEST** Concealed amongst ground vegetation on grassy or marshy areas.

breeding

★★★ **Pectoral Sandpiper** *Calidris melanotos*

| s | s | **A** | w | MARSH

Rare passage migrant, mainly in autumn. from N America or possibly Siberia. **ID** Recalls smaller version of Ruff, especially when stretches up neck if alarmed. Scaly upperparts with pale stripes on back; throat and breast finely streaked with distinct pectoral band giving way to white belly; pale yellowish legs. In flight recalls Ruff, with indistinct pale wing bar and white ovals at base of tail. **VOICE** A short trill.

★ **Dunlin** *Calidris alpina*

| **S** | **S** | **A** | **W** | COAST, MARSH, MOOR, MOUNTAIN

Fairly common, mainly upland breeder; very common coastal passage migrant and winter visitor from Greenland, Iceland and N Europe. **ID** The most abundant shore wader in winter, often found in large flocks. Length of bill varies according to sex and race, with longest billed breeding in Arctic. In winter grey above and white below. In flight, narrow white wing bar. **VOICE** Flight call a rolling 'treee'. **NEST** On ground in grassy tussock.

breeding

breeding

★★ **Curlew Sandpiper** *Calidris ferruginea*

| **S** | s | **A** | w | MARSH

Scarce visitor from Arctic Siberia, mainly to coastal marshes in autumn. **ID** Slightly larger, longer necked and more upright than Dunlin, with longer, more decurved bill and longer legs. Brick-red head and underparts in breeding plumage. Pale grey in winter. **VOICE** Flight call a very distinctive, liquid 'chirrip'.

★ **Sanderling** *Calidris alba*

| **S** | s | **A** | w | COAST

Fairly common winter visitor from Siberia to sandy coasts. **ID** Small, strikingly pale wader in winter, characteristic of open, sandy beaches; rather short, stout bill. In breeding plumage, rufous upper breast sharply demarcated from white underparts. In winter pale grey. In flight, very distinct long, white wing bar. Runs back and forth following the ebb and flow of the waves. **VOICE** Flight call a liquid 'quit-quit'.

breeding

★ **Common Sandpiper** *Actitis hypoleucos*

| S | S | A | W | COAST, FRESH, MOOR

Common but localised summer visitor; rare in winter. **ID** Horizontal carriage and longish tail. Flies low over water; shallow, flicked wing beats alternating with brief glides on down-curved wings. Constantly bobs tail end while walking or resting. **VOICE** Flight call a run of 5-6 high-pitched, piping notes, 'twee-wee-wee-wee...'. Song a rhythmically repeated series of similar calls. **NEST** On open ground or amongst vegetation, close to water.

breeding

★★ **Green Sandpiper** *Tringa ochropus*

| S | S | A | W | FRESH, MARSH

breeding

Fairly common passage migrant and scarce winter visitor from N Europe; has bred occasionally. **ID** Very dark brown, almost black upperparts and breast; greenish legs. In flight, looks like an outsized House Martin with a prominent, square white rump and dark underwing. A rather shy wader, easily flushed, that bobs like a Common Sandpiper. **VOICE** In flight gives a clear, ringing 'tluee, wee, wee' with an upward inflection at the start. **NEST** Usually on the ground.

★★ **Wood Sandpiper** *Tringa glareola*

| S | S | A | W | FRESH, MARSH

Rare summer visitor to Scotland; scarce passage migrant mainly in autumn from N Europe. **ID** Recalls Green Sandpiper but has paler brown upperparts with more speckling, a distinct white 'eyebrow' and longer, yellowish legs. In flight, less contrasting upperparts than Green Sandpiper and pale underwing. **VOICE** Flight call a distinctive 'chiff, chiff, chiff'. **NEST** Usually on ground but occasionally in shrub or tree.

non-breeding

★★ **Little Stint** *Calidris minuta*

| S | S | A | W | COAST, MARSH

Scarce passage migrant, mainly in autumn, from Arctic Norway and Siberia; rare but regular in winter. **ID** Smallest of the common waders, often found in flocks with Dunlin. Dainty; pale V on back; short, straight bill; legs black. In winter grey above and white below. More rapid feeding action than Dunlin. **VOICE** Shrill, high-pitched 'tit'.

breeding

★★★ **Temminck's Stint** *Calidris temminckii* <

| S | S | A | W | MARSH

Rare summer visitor in Scotland and rare passage migrant from N Europe. **ID** More attenuated shape than Little Stint with shorter, pale legs, although these can appear dark when covered with mud. May recall small version of Common Sandpiper in non-breeding plumage. Fairly distinct pectoral band in summer plumage. Shuffles around with a slower feeding action than Little Stint and tends to remain unobtrusively hidden in vegetation. In flight, white outer tail feathers; often towers like a Snipe on being flushed. **VOICE** A distinctive trill.

breeding

★ **Ringed Plover** *Charadrius hiaticula* <

| S | S | A | W | COAST, FARM, FRESH, HEATH

breeding

Fairly common resident and passage migrant from Canada, Greenland, Iceland and Fennoscandia. **ID** One of the most characteristic breeding birds of our coasts, easily recognised by broad black breast band; orange bill and legs. Long winged in flight with prominent but narrow white wing bar. Butterfly-like display flight while giving song. Runs rapidly with brief pauses. **VOICE** Flight call a distinct, soft, disyllabic 'too, lee'. Song a fairly rapid, mellow series of trilling flight calls. **NEST** On ground on sand, shingle or bare ground near water.

★★ **Little Ringed Plover** *Charadrius dubius* <

| S | S | A | W | FRESH, MARSH

Scarce summer visitor in England and Wales. **ID** Slimmer, more attenuated shape than Ringed Plover and legs appear longer. Yellow eye ring, all black bill and pale legs. In flight, no wing bar. **VOICE** Flight call 'peeoo' with downward inflection at end, a run of which is given during its bat-like display flight. **NEST** Shallow scrape on bare ground or amongst short grass.

breeding

93

★★ **Great Skua**
Stercorarius skua

| S | S | A | W | COAST, MOOR |

Fairly common summer visitor to coastal and island colonies in Scotland, and elsewhere to coastal waters, mainly in autumn. **ID** Largest skua, the size of Herring Gull; dark brown with distinct white patches on upper and underwings; minimal central tail projections. Kills and eats birds, as well as chasing seabirds for disgorged food. Also known as Bonxie. **NEST** Depression in grass, heather or moss.

★★ **Pomarine Skua**
Stercorarius pomarinus

| S | S | A | W | COAST |

Scarce visitor from Arctic, mainly in autumn to coastal waters in S and W. **ID** Between Arctic and Great Skuas in size; heavy chested. Dark form brown, more likely to be mistaken for Great Skua, due to broad wings and slow flight; pale form white below. Both forms have spoon-shaped tail projections in fresh breeding plumage. Chases other seabirds until food is disgorged, which is then caught in mid-air (known as 'kleptoparasitism').

pale form

dark form

pale form

dark form

★ Arctic Skua
Stercorarius parasiticus

| S | S | A | W | COAST, MOOR |

Fairly common summer visitor to coastal and island colonies in Scotland, and elsewhere to coastal waters, mainly in autumn. **ID** Gull-like seabird with more pointed wings and dashing, falcon-like flight. Dark form brown. Pale form brown above and white below; intermediate plumages also occur. In flight, narrower wings with less distinct white flashes than Pomarine Skua; also has elongated, pointed central tail feathers in fresh breeding plumage. Feeds by kleptoparasitism (see above). **NEST** Shallow depression in grass, heather or moss.

★★★ Long-tailed Skua
Stercorarius longicaudus

| S | S | A | W | COAST |

Generally a rare autumn visitor from Arctic and N Europe to coastal waters, mainly in S and E England; spring passage migrant past Outer Hebrides. **ID** Rarest and smallest of the four skuas, with long, slim wings recalling tern. Dark above and white below with extremely long central tail feathers in fresh breeding plumage. Feeds from surface of sea, as well as chasing other seabirds for disgorged food.

pale form

★ **Mute Swan** *Cygnus olor*

1st winter

| S | S | A | W | FARM, FRESH, MARSH

Common and widespread lowland resident. **ID** The familiar swan of our park lakes is the largest bird in Britain and Ireland; long neck is either held straight or in a gentle curve. Adult white with orange bill. Feeds by upending, when the long pointed tail is visible; adopts a threatening posture with wings arched like sails and head lowered over back, known as 'busking'. **VOICE** Hissing noise when being aggressive. In flight wings produce a pulsating sound. **NEST** High mound of reeds or other vegetation on or by water's edge.

★★ **Whooper Swan** *Cygnus cygnus* >

| S | S | A | W | FARM, FRESH, MARSH

Rare breeder in Scotland; fairly common winter visitor from N Europe and Iceland to many traditional sites, mainly in N and W. **ID** Larger than Bewick's Swan, neck appears longer and straighter than Mute Swan. Adult white with largely yellow bill. Not always easy to separate from Bewick's Swan in flight. Migrates and winters in family groups. **VOICE** The most vocal swan, with loud, bugling calls, often given in groups of 3-4.

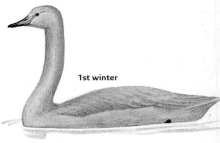

1st winter

★★ **Bewick's Swan** *Cygnus columbianus* >

| S | S | A | W | FARM, FRESH, MARSH

Fairly common winter visitor from Siberia to scattered, often traditional, locations, mainly in S and W. **ID** Smallest and daintiest of our three swans with comparatively short, straight neck; a smaller version of Whooper Swan. Adult white with small rounded yellow area at base of largely black bill. Not always easy to separate from Whooper Swan in flight, but smaller with shorter neck. Migrates and winters in family groups. **VOICE** Higher pitched and more yelping than Whooper Swan, with notes given singly or at most in twos.

1st winter

⋆ Canada Goose
Branta canadensis

| S | S | A | W | FARM, FRESH, MARSH

Common and widespread introduced resident throughout most of England. **ID** Large, long-necked goose; white chin strap contrasting with black head and neck. In flight, long wings and long neck. Individuals of the smaller races of Canada Geese are increasingly being reported in winter, often with flocks of grey geese, and are almost certainly genuinely wild vagrants. **VOICE** Deep, musical honking. **NEST** Near water's edge, often on island and partly hidden.

⋆ Brent Goose *Branta bernicla* <

| S | S | A | W | COAST, FARM, MARSH

Very common winter visitor from Siberia and Greenland, mainly to S and E coasts and Ireland. **ID** Smallest goose, about size of Mallard; generally dark appearance; white neck collar visible at close range. In winter grazes in large, closely packed flocks, often with Wigeon. **VOICE** Distinctive chattering, guttural calls.

dark form

⋆⋆⋆ Snow Goose
Anser caerulescens

| S | S | A | W | FARM, MARSH

Rare visitor from N America, but feral birds frequently occur. **ID** Dark form (known as Blue Goose) mainly dark with white restricted to head, upper neck and tip of tail. White form entirely white apart from black primaries. **VOICE** An unusual soft cackling.

★ Greylag Goose
Anser anser

| S | S | A | W | FARM, FRESH, MARSH

Common winter visitor from Iceland to Scotland; elsewhere fairly common resident feral populations. **ID** Large, bulky goose; grey tone to plumage with no contrast between body and head and neck; orange bill and pink legs, although bill may appear pink in certain lights. In flight, very pale grey upper and under forewing, and pale grey rump contrasting with darker brown back and inner wing. **VOICE** Loud cackling, similar to farmyard geese. **NEST** On ground, often in an exposed position and in a loose colony. The only genuinely wild grey goose to breed in Britain and Ireland.

★★ Bean Goose
Anser fabalis

| S | S | A | W | FARM, MARSH

Scarce winter visitor, mainly in SE, from N Europe and Siberia. **ID** Rarest of the regular grey geese in Britain and Ireland; large, long-necked, dark-looking goose; orange legs and bill, although bill may appear pink in certain lights. Appear long-winged in flight, with dark upper and underwings. Remains in family groups during winter. **VOICE** Deep trumpeting calls, lower pitched than Pink-footed Goose.

★ Pink-footed Goose
Anser brachyrhynchus

| S | S | **A** | **W** | COAST, FARM, MARSH |

Very common winter visitor from Arctic to scattered traditional sites. **ID** Small goose, short dark neck and dark head; pink legs and small black bill with pink band. Many adults have a blue-grey tinge to upperparts. In flight, short neck and dark head noticeable; pale upperwing and back. In winter often occurs in vast flocks, but individuals remain in family groups within flock. **VOICE** Rather harsh, high-pitched ringing calls, best remembered as 'pink, pink'.

★ White-fronted Goose
Anser albifrons

| S | S | A | **W** | FARM, MARSH |

Common winter visitor from NE Europe to scattered traditional localities. **ID** A short-necked goose with orange legs. Adult has distinct white patch at base of bill and variable black bars on belly. In flight, dark upperwing and black bars often visible on belly. Tends to occur in smaller flocks than Pink-footed Goose, but remains in family groups during winter. **VOICE** High-pitched, rather musical yelping calls, recalling a pack of small dogs.

★ **Common Scoter** *Melanitta nigra*

| S | S | A | W | COAST

female

Rare localised breeder in Scotland and Ireland; common winter visitor from Iceland and Scandinavia to coastal waters. **ID** The commonest sea duck off the coasts of England, Wales and Ireland. Both sexes mainly dark, but female has paler cheek. Drake all black. Rests in dense rafts on the sea, often diving to feed in unison, with small leap before submerging. Dips head on wing shaking. **NEST** On ground near freshwater lake or pool.

★★ **Velvet Scoter** *Melanitta fusca*

| S | S | A | W | COAST

female

Fairly common winter visitor from N Europe to coastal waters, mainly in E. **ID** Longer and bulkier than Common Scoter; large wedge-shaped bill; white inner wing panel often visible on closed wing. Female often has pale patch on cheek. Drake black. In flight, both sexes appear black with white inner wing panel. Dives by slipping under water without a leap.

★ **Tufted Duck** *Aythya fuligula*

| S | S | A | W | FRESH

female

Fairly common breeder on lowland waters; common winter visitor from N Europe and Iceland to inland waters. **ID** Commonest diving duck breeding in Britain and Ireland. Female generally shows small tuft on nape and some have small white area at base of bill (recalling female Scaup) but black tip to bill is more obvious. Drake black with white flanks. In flight, both sexes show broad white wing bar. **NEST** Under low shrub near water.

★★ **Scaup** *Aythya marila*

| S | S | A | W | COAST

Fairly common winter visitor, mainly from Iceland, to estuarine and coastal waters. **ID** Marine equivalent of Tufted Duck, but slightly larger with a more rounded head. Female shows extensive white at base of bill and a very small black tip to bill. Drake black, pale grey and white. In flight, both sexes show broad white wing bar.

female

★ **Pintail** *Anas acuta*

S S A W FRESH, MARSH

Rare breeder at scattered localities; common winter visitor from N Europe and Siberia, mainly to the larger estuaries. **ID** Slim and elegant compared with other wildfowl. Female all brown with uniform buff-coloured head and grey bill. Feeds by upending. **NEST** Among low vegetation near water.

male

★★ **Garganey** *Anas querquedula*

S S A W FRESH

Scarce summer visitor to scattered localities. **ID** Small, slightly built dabbling duck; size of Teal but bill longer. Female all brown with pale 'eyebrow' and pale spot at base of bill. Feeds by dipping head or skimming surface; unobtrusive and easily overlooked. **VOICE** Crackling display call. **NEST** Concealed in long grass or rushes near water.

male

★★ **Goldeneye** *Bucephala clangula*

S S A W COAST, FRESH

Rare localised breeder inland in Scotland; fairly common winter visitor from Scandinavia to both coastal and inland waters. **ID** Large, rounded head with peaked crown; small bill and yellow iris; white inner wing panel often visible on closed wing. Drake has glossy green head with white patch at base of bill, white breast and flanks. Dives frequently when feeding. **NEST** In hole in tree, or in nesting box.

female

★ **Little Grebe**
Tachybaptus ruficollis

<

| S | S | A | W | FRESH

Common and widespread resident of lowland waters. **ID** Smallest and dumpiest grebe; short neck and bill; fluffed-up rear end. Chestnut cheeks and neck in summer. In flight, uniformly dark back and upperwings. Swims buoyantly, but if disturbed may submerge, leaving only head showing, or may dive and disappear among waterside vegetation. **VOICE** High-pitched trills given by pair in unison. **NEST** Amongst waterside vegetation.

non-breeding

★ **Pochard** *Aythya ferina*

| S | S | A | W | FRESH

Scarce breeder; common winter visitor from Central Europe. **ID** Distinctive peaked crown and sloping forehead forming sweeping curve along top of bill. Drake has chestnut head and grey body. In flight, pale grey wing bar. Gregarious diving duck, rarely found alone. **NEST** Pile of plant material in waterside vegetation.

female

★★★ Red-crested Pochard
Netta rufina

| S | S | A | W | FRESH |

Genuine wild birds are rare visitors from S and E Europe; small numbers of feral birds breed mainly in S and E. **ID** One of the largest freshwater diving ducks. Female has similar head pattern to female Common Scoter, but body is paler. Drake has bright orange head and red bill. In flight, broad white wing bar.

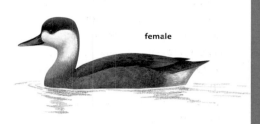

female

★★ Long-tailed Duck
Clangula hyemalis

| S | S | A | W | COAST |

Fairly common winter visitor from Arctic to coastal waters, mainly in N. **ID** Unique amongst wildfowl in having three moults a year, therefore a variety of plumages, with winter drake showing the most white. In flight, both sexes have all-dark wings.

female

★★ Ruddy Duck
Oxyura jamaicensis

<

| S | S | A | W | FRESH |

Native American species that spread following escape from Slimbridge in 1957, now a scarce resident, mainly in the Midlands. **ID** Small and compact with a longish tail, often cocked (thus known as a 'stiff tail'). In breeding plumage drake is chestnut with white cheek and pale blue bill. Gives small leap before diving to feed or escape danger. **NEST** On floating platform in dense aquatic vegetation.

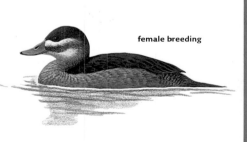

female breeding

★ **Mallard** *Anas platyrhynchos*

| S | S | A | W | FARM, FRESH, MARSH

Very common resident; winter visitor from Scandinavia and Iceland.
ID The familiar duck of urban parks. Female has dull
yellowish bill, orange legs and off-white sides to tail.
Drake has iridescent green head. In flight, purple inner
wing panel with white borders. Feeds by dabbling on
surface and upending. **VOICE** Typical duck's quacking.
NEST Usually amongst ground vegetation.

female

★★ **Gadwall** *Anas strepera*

| S | S | A | W | FRESH

female

Scarce breeder, mainly in S; fairly common in winter. **ID** White inner wing
panel often visible on closed wing and distinct in flight. Female all brown
and very similar to female Mallard but head greyer, bill more orange and
lacks white sides to tail. Drake has grey body with black
rear end. Surface feeder, frequently in small groups.
VOICE Drake gives dry, croaking call, not unlike Mallard.
NEST On ground in thick vegetation near water.

★ **Pintail** *Anas acuta*

| S | S | A | W | FRESH, MARSH

Rare breeder at scattered localities; common winter visitor from N Europe and
Siberia mainly to the larger estuaries. **ID** Slim and elegant compared with other
wildfowl. Female all brown with uniform buff-coloured head
and grey bill. Drake has chocolate-brown head with white
vertical stripe up side of neck. In flight, green inner wing
panel not easily seen but distinct white trailing edge. Feeds
by upending. **NEST** Amongst low vegetation near water.

female

★ **Shoveler** *Anas clypeata*

| S | S | A | W | FRESH

female

Fairly common resident; winter visitor from N Europe. **ID** Both sexes
characterised by large, spatulate bill with which they skim the water surface
for food. Drake has iridescent green head. In flight, grey patch on upper
forewing. Usually seen in pairs or small, dense, circling groups
when feeding. **NEST** Hollow in low waterside vegetation.

★ Teal *Anas crecca*

S | S | A | W | FRESH, MARSH

Fairly common breeder mainly in N and W; very common winter visitor from N Europe and Siberia. **ID** Our smallest duck. Female has white streak under tail. Drake has chestnut head with green mask and yellow triangle on rear flank. In flight, pale mid-wing bar at distance appearing as pale spot in centre of otherwise uniform upperwing. Feeds by upending and leaps from water on taking off, hence the collective noun a 'spring' of Teal. **VOICE** Very vocal when displaying in groups, giving a high-pitched, chirruping call. **NEST** Well concealed on ground.

female

★★ Garganey *Anas querquedula*

S | S | A | W | FRESH

Scarce summer visitor to scattered localities. **ID** Small, slightly built dabbling duck; size of Teal but bill longer. Female has pale 'eyebrow' and spot at base of bill. Drake unmistakable with brown head and broad white 'eyebrow' extending to nape. In flight, grey upper forewing and dark inner wing panel bordered with white but broader along trailing edge of wing. Feeds by dipping head or skimming surface; unobtrusive and easily overlooked. **VOICE** Crackling display call. **NEST** Concealed in long grass or rushes near water.

female

★ Eider *Somateria mollissima*

S | S | A | W | COAST

Common coastal resident in N; smaller numbers also winter in coastal waters of S and E. **ID** Large, short-necked, heavy-looking duck; distinct profile due to long, wedge-shaped bill merging into flat, sloping forehead. Drake black and white. **VOICE** Drake gives a loud 'oooo' with an upward inflection at end, as if surprised. **NEST** On ground amongst rocks, fairly close to sea; nest lined with eider down.

female

★ Green Woodpecker
Picus viridis

| S | S | A | W | FARM, GARDEN, HEATH, PARK, WOOD

Common resident. **ID** Largest of our woodpeckers. Long, powerful, chisel-like bill; white iris; yellow rump visible in flight, when it can be mistaken for a female Golden Oriole, but Green Woodpecker is much larger. Female lacks red centre to stripe below the eye. Feeds on ground on ants. Formerly known as the Yaffle due to far-carrying, laughing call. **VOICE** Loud, ringing, rather hollow echoing calls in runs, 'coo, co, coo...'. **NEST** In hole in tree.

male

male

female

★★★ Golden Oriole
Oriolus oriolus

| S | S | A | W | FRESH, WOOD

Rare summer visitor, mainly to E Anglia. **ID** Despite bright colours of male, can be surprisingly difficult to see amongst the foliage in the tops of the trees (usually poplars) that it frequents, and so is less often seen than heard. Male unmistakable, females variable, some being almost as bright as males, others greener with streaky underparts. **VOICE** Harsh Jay-like calls and cat-like miaows. Song a loud, fluting wolf-whistle ending with 'orioleole'. **NEST** Suspended between two adjacent branches or in the fork of a tree, high in the canopy.

★★ Rose-ringed Parakeet
Psittacula krameri

| S | S | A | W | GARDEN, PARK, WOOD

Fairly common but localised introduced resident. **ID** Fast-flying, long-tailed, noisy, green parrot. Bright red bill. Female head and neck all green. Also known as Ring-necked Parakeet. **VOICE** Loud squawking. **NEST** In hole in tree.

male

★★ Waxwing *Bombycilla garrulus* >

| S | S | A | W | FARM, GARDEN

Scarce to fairly common but unpredictable winter visitor from N and E Europe. **ID** Rotund Starling-sized bird with a thick crest. Bright yellow tips to flight feathers and tail, and sealing-wax-red tips to secondaries, duller in female. Gregarious and approachable, but always remains wary while feeding on berries or fruit, e.g. cotoneaster, rowan and pyracantha. **VOICE** Distinctive ringing trill, likened to a small bell; once heard never forgotten.

★★ Shorelark
Eremophila alpestris >

| S | S | A | W | COAST, FARM, MOUNTAIN

Scarce autumn passage migrant and winter visitor from N Europe; has bred on Scottish mountain tops. **ID** Distinct black and yellow head pattern at all seasons. Female duller than male. Also known as the Horned Lark due to short black 'horns', most noticeable in male in breeding plumage. **VOICE** Flight call like that of Meadow Pipit, a short single or double 'psee, psee'. **NEST** In hollow on ground, often in shelter of a stone or tuft of vegetation.

male breeding

male

★ **Yellowhammer** *Emberiza citrinella*

| S | S | A | W | FARM, HEATH, SCRUB

Abundant but declining resident. **ID** Chestnut rump and conspicuous white outer tail feathers visible as bird flies away. Female duller and more streaked. Often perches conspicuously on top of bush, tree or wires. **VOICE** Flight call a single, metallic 'chip' or double 'pit, pit'. Song the familiar 'a little bit of bread and no cheeeese'. **NEST** Well concealed in grass or vegetation at base of hedge or on side of overgrown bank.

★★ **Crossbill** *Loxia curvirostra*

| S | S | A | W | HEATH, WOOD

Fairly common resident and occasional passage migrant in varying numbers. **ID** Unpredictable and often elusive. Resembles and behaves like a small parrot but with crossed mandibles. Male brick-red. Feeds acrobatically in conifers, sidling along branches and moving from twig to twig by using its bill. Highly gregarious; presence often betrayed by falling pine cones. **VOICE** Distinctive 'chip-chip' contact calls. Song a mixture of trills, twitters and contact calls. **NEST** In conifer, often at a considerable height from ground.

female

male

★★ **Cirl Bunting** *Emberiza cirlus*

| S | S | A | W | FARM

Scarce and localised resident. **ID** Male recalls Yellowhammer but with black eye stripe and throat, and olive-green breast band; also rump olive-brown not chestnut. Female very similar to female Yellowhammer but with olive-grey rump and suggestion of male's darker face markings. **VOICE** Call a sharp 'sip'. Song recalls Lesser Whitethroat, being a short but continuous rattle on a single note. **NEST** Low down in hedge or thick bush.

★ Yellow Wagtail *Motacilla flava*

| S | S | A | W | FARM, FRESH, MARSH

Common but declining summer visitor. **ID** The most pipit-like of the wagtails. Spring males unmistakable with their bright Canary-yellow underparts, females washed-out yellowish below. Various races occur throughout Europe, the males being recognised by their different-coloured head markings: crown, 'eyebrow', cheek and throat. In addition to *M.f.flavissima* that breeds in Britain and Ireland, the Blue-headed Wagtail (*M.f.flava*) breeds in much of W Europe. **VOICE** Flight call a thin 'tsweep'. Song very brief and unmelodic consisting of 2–3 rasping notes. **NEST** Well concealed in long grass or thick ground vegetation.

Blue-headed male

Yellow male

★ Grey Wagtail
Motacilla cinerea

| S | S | A | W | BUILDINGS, FARM, FRESH, MOOR, MOUNTAIN

Common resident and partial migrant. **ID** Graceful, long-tailed wagtail, a typical bird of fast-flowing streams and rivers. Yellow most intense on upper breast and undertail coverts; legs brownish-pink (all other wagtails' legs are black). Female duller. Clear white central wing bar visible from above and below in flight. While perched or walking constantly pumps tail up and down. **VOICE** Flight call more metallic than Pied Wagtail, a sharp 'tzi, tzi'. Song a series of flight calls strung together. **NEST** By waterside, in crevice of bank, amongst roots of tree or in hole in wall, bridge or other building.

male breeding

★ **Greenfinch** *Carduelis chloris*

| S | S | A | W | FARM, GARDEN, PARK, SCRUB, WOOD

Very common resident; fairly common winter visitor from N Europe, mainly Norway. **ID** A bulky finch with a fairly heavy, triangular bill; yellow in wings and tail. Female duller than male with some darker streaks on upperparts. Butterfly-like display flight with male flying in circles while singing. **VOICE** Flight call a soft 'chup', also gives a buzzing 'dzweee' while perched. Song a Canary-like trill mixed with twittering. **NEST** In fork of tree or bush.

male

★ **Goldfinch** *Carduelis carduelis*

| S | S | A | W | FARM, GARDEN, PARK, SCRUB, WOOD

Very common and increasing resident and partial migrant. **ID** Unusually pointed bill for a finch; yellow wing bar. Male and female very similar, but male a little brighter with more extensive red on face. Feeds on thistles and teasels. **VOICE** Cheerful, trisyllabic flight call: 'swit, wit, wit'. Song a mixture of rapid trills and twitters, incorporating the flight call. **NEST** In crown of tree, often on thinner, outer branch.

★ **Siskin** *Carduelis spinus*

| S | S | A | W | FRESH, GARDEN, HEATH, MOUNTAIN, WOOD

Very common but localised resident and partial migrant; fairly common winter visitor from N Europe. **ID** Broad yellow wing bars, yellow in tail and on rump; sharply pointed bill. Female a duller, streaky version of male. Feeds at top of birches and alders, often with redpolls. **VOICE** Distinct squeaky, disyllabic call with rising inflection at end. Song a pleasing mixture of trills and twitters. **NEST** Usually near end of a branch of a conifer.

female

male

★ **Blue Tit** *Cyanistes caeruleus* <

| S | S | A | W | FARM, GARDEN, PARK, WOOD

Abundant resident. **ID** One of our most familiar garden birds. Sexes similar but male brighter blue on head and wings. **VOICE** Call a fine 'tsee, tsee, tsee' and scolding churr. Brief and uninspiring song based on calls and finishing with a trill. **NEST** In hole or cavity in tree or brickwork, or a nest box.

★ **Great Tit** *Parus major*

| S | S | A | W | FARM, GARDEN, PARK, WOOD

Abundant resident. **ID** Largest of our tits. Black and white head pattern; black vertical band along centre of yellow underparts, narrower and duller on female. **VOICE** Calls are rich and varied, no two individuals sounding exactly alike. Contact notes very similar to Chaffinch's 'spink' or Marsh Tit's 'tchair, tchair'. Commonest song is a variation on 'teacher, teacher, teacher', recalling the sound of a bicycle tyre being pumped up. **NEST** In hole in tree, brickwork or other man-made object, or a nest box.

★ **Chiffchaff** *Phylloscopus collybita*

`S` `S` `A` `W` FARM, WOOD

Very common summer visitor; scarce winter visitor.
ID Very similar to Willow Warbler, but appears shorter
and less sleek. Very short winged with tip of closed wing
barely reaching base of tail; browner above and buffer
below than Willow Warbler; dark legs. In autumn shows
yellowish underparts. Very restless and flicks tail down
frequently. **VOICE** Call 'hooeet' with rising inflection at
end. Song the familiar 'chiff, chaff, chiff, chaff, chiff,
chiff, chaff...'. **NEST** Domed structure just above ground
level amongst vegetation or in shrub.

★ **Willow Warbler** *Phylloscopus trochilus* <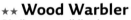

`S` `S` `A` `W` FARM, HEATH, MOUNTAIN, WOOD

Abundant but declining summer visitor. **ID** Our
commonest summer visitor. Very similar to Chiffchaff but
appears sleeker and is longer winged, with tip of closed
wing reaching well down length of tail; distinct yellowish
'eyebrow'; orange at base of lower mandible; legs pale
pinkish-brown. **VOICE** Call a disyllabic, soft 'hooit'.
Song a beautiful liquid cascade with a terminal flourish.
NEST Domed structure on ground amongst vegetation.

★★ **Wood Warbler**
Phylloscopus sibilatrix

`S` `S` `A` `W` WOOD

Fairly common summer visitor, mainly in uplands.
ID Appears larger, longer winged and shorter tailed
than Willow Warbler. Bright yellow breast sharply
demarcated from pure white belly. Sings with head
raised and body quivering. **VOICE** Song a slowly
repeated series of single notes accelerating to a
shivering trill, also a run of piping notes repeated
up to about 20 times. **NEST** Domed structure
amongst ground vegetation.

★★★ Yellow-browed Warbler
Phylloscopus inornatus

| s | s | **A** | w | COAST, SCRUB, WOOD

Rare autumn passage migrant from Siberia. **ID** A little larger than the Goldcrests with which it often feeds. Long creamy 'eyebrow', double wing bar, pale edges to innermost wing feathers. Constantly on the move, even more restless than Goldcrest. **VOICE** A surprisingly loud and penetrating call for so small a bird, not dissimilar to a Coal Tit – 'tsweest', with rising inflection at end.

★ Goldcrest *Regulus regulus*

| **S** | **S** | **A** | **W** | GARDEN, MOUNTAIN, WOOD

Very common resident and partial migrant; fairly common autumn passage migrant and winter visitor, mainly from Scandinavia. **ID** Our smallest bird, and one of the characteristic species of coniferous woods. Central crown stripe appears yellow in both sexes, unless male is excited, when concealed red feathers are exposed; double white wing bars. Feeds in manner of warbler, never still and often very confiding. Joins mixed tit flocks outside breeding season. **VOICE** Call a thin, high-pitched 'tzee, tzee, tzee', the notes tending to be slurred together. Song a series of thin calls with a terminal trill. **NEST** In fork or suspended under foliage near end of conifer branch.

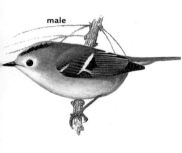

male

★★ Firecrest *Regulus ignicapilla*

| **S** | **S** | **A** | **W** | COAST, SCRUB, WOOD

Rare breeder and partial migrant; scarce passage migrant and winter visitor from Europe. **ID** Size of Goldcrest but more brightly marked. Prominent white 'eyebrow'; black crown stripes meet above orange-buff forehead; bright golden bronze patch on collar and shoulder; silky white underparts. Male has orange central crown stripe that is usually visible in field **VOICE** A little more strident and lower pitched than Goldcrest, 'zi, zi, zi', each note being separate. **NEST** As Goldcrest.

male

113

★★ Marsh Harrier
Circus aeruginosus

Female

| S | S | A | W | FARM, MARSH, REEDS

Scarce but increasing resident and summer visitor.
ID Narrower wings and longer tail than Common
Buzzard, but broader wings than other harriers. Male
has contrasting grey, brown and black wings. Rather
lazy, low, quartering flight; also soars high in air with
wings raised in shallow V. **NEST** On platform of dead
vegetation in reedbed or on ground amongst cereal
or arable crops.

★ Golden Plover *Pluvialis apricaria*

| S | S | A | W | COAST, FARM, MARSH, MOOR, MOUNTAIN

Common upland breeder; very common lowland winter
visitor from Iceland and N Europe. **ID** Smaller, less stout
than Grey Plover. Spangled golden upperparts in
summer. Black face and underparts variable according
to sex and race, absent outside breeding season.
Rather shy and always alert, favouring drier areas for
feeding. In winter gathers into very large flocks, usually
on arable land, and often mixed with Lapwings. **VOICE**
Distinct, plaintive flight call: 'too'. Song a penetrating,
rippling trill. **NEST** On ground amongst heather.

breeding

★ Teal *Anas crecca*

| S | S | A | W | FRESH, MARSH

Fairly common breeder in N and W; very common winter visitor
from N Europe and Siberia. **ID** Our smallest duck. Drake has
horizontal white stripe along flank, yellow triangle on rear flank
and green eye patch outlined in yellow. Female all brown.
Feeds by upending and leaps from water on taking off,
hence the collective noun a 'spring' of Teal. **VOICE**
Very vocal when displaying in groups, giving a
high-pitched, chirruping call. **NEST** Well
concealed in ground vegetation.

male

★ **Wigeon** *Anas penelope*

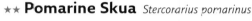

| S | S | **A** | **W** | FRESH, MARSH

Scarce breeder mainly in N; very common winter visitor from N Europe and Siberia. **ID** Adult drake shows yellow central crown stripe and white wing patch in flight. Female has variable chestnut underparts. Grazing ducks often form large winter flocks and join Brent Geese on coastal saltings and marshes. **VOICE** Drake gives characteristic drawn-out whistle. **NEST** On ground in thick waterside vegetation.

male

★★ **Pomarine Skua** *Stercorarius pomarinus*

| S | S | **A** | **W** | COAST

pale form

Scarce visitor from Arctic, mainly in autumn to coastal waters in S and W. **ID** Between Arctic and Great Skuas in size; heavy-chested. Pale form has more complete dark breast band than Arctic Skua, more extensive yellow on face and heavier bill with pink base. Dark form all brown, apart from distinct wing flashes. Chases other seabirds until victim disgorges food, which is then caught in mid-air (known as 'kleptoparasitism').

★ **Gannet** *Morus bassanus*

| S | S | **A** | **W** | COAST

Very common breeder in a few scattered colonies around N and W coasts; elsewhere fairly common in coastal waters, especially in autumn. **ID** Large black and white seabird with heavy dagger-like bill. Adult has ochre flush on head in breeding season. **NEST** In gannetries on ground or rocky ledge.

breeding

★★★ **Spoonbill** *Platalea leucorodia*

| S | S | **A** | W | FRESH, MARSH

Rare summer visitor; has bred in England. **ID** Large all-white wading bird; long bill with spoon-shaped tip; long, drooping crest and ochre breast band present only in breeding season. **NEST** In trees and reedbeds.

★ **Mallard** *Anas platyrhynchos*

S S A W FARM, FRESH, MARSH

Very common resident; winter visitor from Scandinavia and Iceland. **ID** The familiar duck of urban parks; yellow bill and orange legs. Only drake has iridescent green head. Female all brown. Feeds by dabbling on surface and upending. **VOICE** Typical duck's quacking. **NEST** Usually well concealed amongst ground vegetation.

male

★ **Shoveler** *Anas clypeata*

S S A W FRESH

male

Fairly common resident; winter visitor from N Europe. **ID** Both sexes characterised by large, spatulate bill with which they skim the water surface for food. Only drake has iridescent green head. Female all brown. Usually seen in pairs or small, dense, circling groups when feeding. **NEST** Hollow in low waterside vegetation.

★ **Shelduck** *Tadorna tadorna*

S S A W COAST, FARM, FRESH, HEATH, MARSH

Common resident around coasts and estuaries, also breeding inland. **ID** One of the most conspicuous and colourful estuarine birds; can appear black and white at a distance. Both sexes have iridescent green head. **VOICE** Drake gives characteristic hissing whistle in flight, female a nagging, guttural call. **NEST** Usually in underground burrow.

male

★ **Goosander** *Mergus merganser*

S S A W FRESH

Fairly common breeder on rivers and inland waters in N and W, spreading further south in winter. **ID** Large, long heavy body; long red bill with hooked tip. At a distance drake appears black and white. Female has brown head and grey body. **NEST** In hole in tree, bank or amongst boulders near water.

male

★ Red-breasted Merganser
Mergus serrator

| S | S | A | W | COAST, FRESH

Fairly common breeder in freshwater and tidal habitats in N and W, moving to coastal waters in winter. **ID** Smaller and slimmer than Goosander; shaggy crest; finer bill. Female has brown head and grey body. **NEST** Concealed under vegetation or boulder near water.

male

★ Teal *Anas crecca*

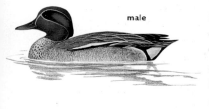

male

| S | S | A | W | FRESH, MARSH

Fairly common breeder mainly in N and W; very common winter visitor from N Europe and Siberia. **ID** Our smallest duck. Drake has horizontal white stripe along flank. Female all brown. Feeds by upending and leaps from water on taking off, hence the collective noun a 'spring' of Teal. **VOICE** Very vocal when displaying in groups, giving a high-pitched, chirruping call. **NEST** Well concealed in ground vegetation.

★ Eider *Somateria mollissima*

| S | S | A | W | COAST

Common coastal resident in N; smaller numbers also winter in coastal waters of S and E. **ID** Large, short-necked, heavy-looking duck; distinct profile due to long, wedge-shaped bill merging into flat, sloping forehead. Female all brown; eclipse (post-breeding) drakes show varying amounts of white. In flight, adult drake is black and white. **VOICE** Drake gives a loud 'oooo' with an upward inflection at end, as if surprised. **NEST** On ground amongst rocks, fairly close to sea; nest lined with eider down.

male breeding

★★ **Black Grouse** *Tetrao tetrix*

male

`s` `s` `A` `w` FARM, HEATH, MOOR, WOOD

Localised and declining resident. **ID** Male has strange lyre-shaped tail and purplish gloss in sun. Female brown, barred darker, some with notched tail. Male also known as Blackcock and female as Greyhen. **VOICE** Male gives bubbling calls, audible at long range. **NEST** On ground amongst low plants.

★★ **Raven** *Corvus corax*

`s` `s` `A` `w` COAST, FARM, MOOR, MOUNTAIN, WOOD

Fairly common but localised resident. **ID** Our largest crow, even bigger than a Buzzard. All-black plumage but green or bluish gloss in sun. Very heavy bill; shaggy throat feathers. Pairs for life and often seen with partner. **VOICE** Deep, croaking call, recalling a distant dog barking. **NEST** On rock ledge or in fork of tree.

★ **Carrion Crow** *Corvus corone*

`s` `s` `A` `w` FARM, HEATH, MOOR, PARK, WOOD

Abundant resident. **ID** All-black plumage but glossy green in sun. Flatter crown than Rook and stouter bill with down-curved lower mandible. Does occur in groups but more often seen singly or in pairs. **VOICE** Usually gives a trisyllabic 'cor, cor, cor'. **NEST** Generally in a fairly tall tree.

★ **Rook** *Corvus frugilegus*

`s` `s` `A` `w` FARM, PARK, WOOD

Abundant resident. **ID** All-black plumage but glossy purple in sun. Peaked crown rising steeply from base of long, narrow, pointed bill; area of bare, whitish skin around base of bill; triangular swelling rising from lower mandible in breeding season only. Gregarious and often found in mixed flocks with Jackdaws. **VOICE** Most vocal at rookery, a loud 'car, car', less harsh than crow. **NEST** In tree-top colonies.

★★ **Chough**
Pyrrhocorax pyrrhocorax

| S | S | A | W | COAST, FARM

Fairly common but very localised resident. **ID** Size of Jackdaw. The only all-black bird with a long, red, decurved bill. Bluish gloss to plumage in sun. Highly sociable and rarely seen alone. Performs acrobatic aerial manoeuvres. **VOICE** Jackdaw-like call but higher pitched 'cheow', from which it gets its name. **NEST** On ledge in cave.

★ **Magpie** *Pica pica*

| S | S | A | W | FARM, GARDEN, SCRUB

Very common resident. **ID** Noisy, black and white bird with a very long tail, especially evident when flying. At closer range and in sun, glossy metallic sheen on wings. Rapid wing beats followed by a brief pause. **VOICE** Well-known alarm call consists of a harsh chattering. **NEST** Domed structure in tree, bush or hedge.

★ **Starling** *Sturnus vulgaris*

| S | S | A | W | BUILDINGS, FARM, GARDEN, PARK, WOOD

Abundant but declining resident and winter visitor. **ID** A gregarious and quarrelsome visitor to many gardens. In summer, appears all black with yellow bill, but purplish-green gloss evident in sun; male has blue base to bill and female pink base and a white iris. Walks rather than hops. **VOICE** Rapid, noisy chattering incorporates the calls of many other local species, e.g. Magpie, House Sparrow, Curlew, etc. **NEST** In hole in tree, wall of building, roof or nest box.

breeding

★ Cormorant *Phalacrocorax carbo*

| S | S | A | W | COAST, FRESH

Common resident around many rocky coasts and at some inland sites; more widespread inland in winter. **ID** Large, heavy looking and long necked; peak of crown at rear of head; strong hooked bill with area of bare, yellowish skin at base. In breeding plumage, bluish gloss to underparts and bronze sheen on closed wings. In flight, uniformly black with white thigh patch in early breeding plumage. Swims low in water when long tail may be visible (compare with divers) and bill held pointing slightly upwards. Often sits on groynes or posts with wings outstretched. **NEST** On cliffs or inland in trees.

breeding

breeding

★ Shag *Phalacrocorax aristotelis*

| S | S | A | W | COAST

Common resident around many rocky coasts, scarce inland. **ID** Smaller and slimmer than Cormorant; smaller, more rounded head with peak of crown above eye and pencil-thin bill. Crest only present in breeding plumage, when green gloss to underparts and purplish sheen to closed wings. In flight, uniformly black. Leaps out of water before diving. **NEST** On cliffs or rocky ledge.

★ Lapwing *Vanellus vanellus*

| S | S | A | W | COAST, FARM, MARSH

Very common but decreasing lowland breeder; abundant winter visitor from N Europe. **ID** One of the characteristic birds of farmland. Appears black and white, but upperparts have greeny-purple iridescence; long, thin, wispy crest; orange vent most visible when the bird tips forward to feed. Tumbling display flight in spring. Often in large flocks out of breeding season. Also known as Peewit and Green Plover. **VOICE** Scolding 'peewee'. **NEST** On ground on field or marshland.

breeding

★ Tufted Duck *Aythya fuligula*

| S | S | A | W | FRESH

Fairly common breeder on lowland waters; common winter visitor from N Europe and Iceland to inland waters. **ID** Commonest diving duck breeding in Britain and Ireland; both sexes have yellow eye. Female dull brown with paler flank. In flight, drake is black and white. **NEST** Under low shrub near water.

male

male

★★ Scaup *Aythya marila*

| S | S | A | W | COAST

Fairly common winter visitor, mainly from Iceland, to estuarine and coastal waters. **ID** Marine equivalent of Tufted Duck; rounded head, yellow eye and grey bill. Female dull brown with paler flank. In flight, drake is black and white.

★★ Goldeneye
Bucephala clangula

<

| S | S | A | W | COAST, FRESH

Rare localised breeder inland in Scotland; fairly common winter visitor from Scandinavia to both coastal and inland waters. **ID** Large, rounded head with peaked crown; small bill and yellow iris; white panel often visible on closed wing. Female has brown head and greyish body. In flight, drake appears black and white. Dives frequently when feeding. **NEST** In hole in tree, or in nest box.

male

★ **Swallow** *Hirundo rustica*

| S | S | A | W | BUILDINGS, FARM, FRESH

Very common summer visitor. **ID** Long, pointed wings and tail streamers. Glossy metallic blue back; red on head visible only at close range; underparts vary from white to chestnut-buff depending on race. Female has shorter tail streamers. **VOICE** Rapid twittering at rest and in flight; shrill alarm call. **NEST** Open mud nest on rafters or ledge in cow shed, stable, outhouse, garage or other building.

male

★ **House Martin** *Delichon urbicum*

| S | S | A | W | BUILDINGS, COAST

Very common summer visitor. **ID** Short, forked tail with no streamers. Glossy blue-black back and head; white rump and underparts; white feathers cover legs and feet. Glides more than Swallow. **VOICE** A chirruping twitter in flight; shrill alarm call. **NEST** Usually in colony, enclosed mud nest with entrance hole near top, built under eaves or locally on cliffs.

★ **Nuthatch** *Sitta europaea*

| S | S | A | W | GARDEN, PARK, WOOD

Very common resident. **ID** Rather dumpy and short tailed, with a dagger-like bill; chestnut flanks brighter on male. Our only bird able to climb down tree trunks headfirst. **VOICE** A variety of calls and songs, including a loud, ringing, oft-repeated 'chwit-chwit-chwit' and a shrill trill. **NEST** In hole in tree, with mud plastered around entrance hole and any crevices in cavity.

★★ **Kingfisher** *Alcedo atthis*

| S | S | A | W | FRESH

Fairly common resident. **ID** One of our most colourful birds, but often smaller than imagined; rather dumpy and short tailed with a long, dagger-shaped bill. Sexes similar but female has reddish base to lower mandible in breeding plumage. Perches upright, but despite bright colours can be remarkably well camouflaged when sitting in shadow; plunges into water to catch small fish, occasionally hovering before diving; flies like an arrow low over water. **VOICE** A piping, metallic 'tzi' in flight. **NEST** In tunnelled hole in sandy bank.

★ **Jay** *Garrulus glandarius*

| S | S | A | W | FARM, GARDEN, PARK, WOOD

Very common resident. **ID** Bright blue wing patch finely barred black; white rump. Raises crown feathers in alarm or display. Often moves around in small, noisy parties. **VOICE** Loud and raucous 'tchaar'. A great mimic; song comprises a bizarre mixture of clicks, mews and chuckles. **NEST** In fork against main trunk of tree.

★★★ **Bluethroat** *Luscinia svecica*

| S | S | A | W | SCRUB

Rare visitor from continental Europe to coastal areas. **ID** Whitish 'eyebrow'; chestnut at base of tail, especially visible in flight. Blue on throat absent or much reduced in female. Actions much as Robin; flicks tail when perched. Two races: Red-spotted (*L.s.svecica*) from N Europe and White-spotted (*L.s.cyanecula*) from S and Central Europe. **VOICE** A sharp 'tac'.

male

male

★ **Chaffinch** *Fringilla coelebs*

| S | S | A | W | FARM, GARDEN, HEATH, PARK, WOOD

Abundant resident and winter visitor mainly from Scandinavia. **ID** One of our most widespread birds and the second commonest. Double white wing bars and white sides to tail. Female plain buffy-grey. In winter sexes often found in separate flocks. **VOICE** Cheerful 'spink' and a difficult to locate 'hooeet'. Song a vigorous cascade with a terminal flourish, tirelessly repeated after a short interval and often followed by a nearby rival's song. **NEST** In fork of tree or bush.

★★★ **Red-backed Shrike**
Lanius collurio

| S | S | A | W | HEATH, SCRUB

Rare summer visitor and passage migrant from N Europe. **ID** Perches in open but can be surprisingly elusive. Female dull rufous-brown above and barred below. When perched often swings tail from side to side; tail appears fairly long in flight. **VOICE** Harsh, grating 'check'. **NEST** In bush or shrub.

male

male

★★ **Bearded Tit** *Panurus biarmicus*

| S | S | A | W | REEDS

Scarce resident and partial migrant. **ID** Lives exclusively in or near reedbeds. Tawny brown bird with a long tail, hence old colloquial name of 'Reed Pheasant'. Female lacks blue head and black moustache, bill usually dark. Whirring flight across tops of reeds, but remains low down in reeds on windy days. **VOICE** Distinctive twanging or pinging calls, given at rest and in flight. **NEST** Low down in reeds, near edge of stand.

male

★★ Blue-headed Wagtail
Motacilla flava

| S | S | A | W | FARM, FRESH, MARSH

Scarce passage migrant from W Europe. **ID** Spring males are distinctive with blue head, long white 'eyebrow' and yellow throat. Female very similar to British and Irish race of Yellow Wagtail, but with a suggestion of the male's head pattern. **VOICE** Flight call a thin 'tsweep'.

★ Great Tit *Parus major*

| S | S | A | W | FARM, GARDEN, PARK, WOOD

Abundant resident. **ID** Largest of our tits. Black and white head pattern; black vertical band along centre of yellow underparts, broader and blacker on male. **VOICE** Calls are rich and varied, no two individuals sounding exactly alike. Contact notes very similar to Chaffinch's 'spink' or Marsh Tit's 'tchair, tchair'. Commonest song a variation on 'teacher, teacher, teacher', recalling the sound of a bicycle tyre being pumped up. **NEST** In hole in tree, brickwork or other man-made object, or a nest box.

★ Blue Tit *Cyanistes caeruleus* <

| S | S | A | W | FARM, GARDEN, PARK, WOOD

Abundant resident. **ID** One of our most familiar garden birds. Sexes similar but female duller blue on head and wings. **VOICE** Call a fine 'tsee, tsee, tsee' and scolding churr. Brief and uninspiring song based on calls and finishing with a trill. **NEST** In hole or cavity in tree or brickwork, or a nest box.

★ **Wood Pigeon** *Columba palumbus*

| S | S | A | W | FARM, GARDEN, SCRUB, WOOD

Abundant resident. **ID** Our largest and bulkiest dove. White patch on sides of neck and white bar across wing in flight. Explodes noisily from cover when disturbed; display flight involves loud wing claps and glides. Highly gregarious at most times of the year. **VOICE** A five-syllable cooing with a gap between the second and third notes. May be remembered as 'I'm a...Wood Pigeon'. **NEST** In tree, bush or hedge.

★ **Stock Dove** *Columba oenas*

| S | S | A | W | BUILDINGS, FARM, GARDEN, PARK, WOOD

Very common resident. **ID** Noticeably smaller and more compact than Wood Pigeon; iridescent patch on sides of neck. In flight can recall small raptor; blackish wing tips; short black wing bars; grey rump (many Feral Pigeons and all true Rock Doves have white rump). Feeds in fields with Wood Pigeons in winter, but on taking flight Stock Doves usually form a separate group. **VOICE** Disyllabic cooing. **NEST** In hole in tree, building or cliff. Several pairs may breed together.

★★ **Rock Dove/★ Feral Pigeon**
Columba livia

| S | S | A | W | BUILDINGS, COAST, FARM

Rock Dove a fairly common resident of coastal cliffs in N and W Britain and Ireland; Feral Pigeon a very common resident. **ID** Rock Dove is paler grey above than Stock Dove with double black wing bar and white rump; also white underwing. Feral Pigeon occurs in a wide variety of plumages from white through grey to almost black, and also pink; generally lacks white rump. **VOICE** Familiar cooing. **NEST** Tend to be colonial. Rock Dove nests in caves or crevices in sea cliffs, Feral Pigeon on ledges on or in buildings.

★ **Hooded Crow** *Corvus cornix*

| S | S | **A** | **W** | FARM, MOOR, PARK, WOOD

Very common resident in Scotland and Ireland; elsewhere scarce winter visitor from Scandinavia. **ID** Otherwise known as Grey Crow. Wide zone of hybridisation between the breeding ranges of Carrion and Hooded Crows. **VOICE** Hoarse croaking as Carrion Crow. **NEST** In tall tree, on cliff ledge or rocky outcrop.

★ **Jackdaw** *Corvus monedula*

| S | S | **A** | **W** | BUILDINGS, COAST, FARM, GARDEN, PARK, WOOD

Very common resident. **ID** Noticeably smaller and dumpier than Rook or Carrion Crow. All dark, although grey nape and cheek, and white iris visible at close range. A jaunty, gregarious bird; forms a life-long bond and is usually seen in pairs; also often in flocks with Rooks. **VOICE** Call an almost musical 'jack'. **NEST** In hole or cavity in tree, building, chimney or cave, in a loose colony.

★★ **Nightjar** *Caprimulgus europaeus*

| S | **S** | A | W | COAST, HEATH, MOOR, WOOD

Fairly common but localised summer visitor. **ID** A characteristic bird of heathland, moorland and clear-fell areas of woodland; crepuscular habits and excellent camouflage make it very difficult to observe well. Falcon-like flight silhouette with long, pointed wings and long, narrow tail. Flies silently except when wing-clapping in courtship display or calling. **VOICE** Unforgettable churring that can continue seemingly for hours at a time from dusk until dawn, especially on calm, balmy nights. Flight call a distinct 'too-ik'. **NEST** Simple hollow on ground, often near piece of old wood.

male

★ Fieldfare *Turdus pilaris*

| S | s | A | W | FARM, MOOR, PARK, WOOD

Rare breeder and abundant winter visitor from
N Europe. **ID** Appears larger than Blackbird,
having longer wings and tail. In flight, pale grey
rump and white underwing (like Mistle Thrush).
Gregarious and often associates with Redwings
and Starlings. Dive-bombs and defecates on
intruders in breeding territory. **VOICE** Flight
calls a chattering 'tchak, tchak, tchak' and a
quieter 'see'. Song a brief, simple chattering.
NEST In fork of tree, usually in loose colony.

**female
Pied Wagtail**

**male
White Wagtail**

★ Pied Wagtail
Motacilla alba

| S | S | A | W | BUILDINGS, FARM, GARDEN,
MARSH

Very common resident and partial migrant.
ID Our only small black and white bird with
a long tail that is constantly wagged up and
down. Adult male has black upperparts;
both sexes have blackish rump. Breeding in
the rest of Europe is the race *M.a.alba*
(White Wagtail), which is a scarce visitor to
Britain and Ireland, and differs from the
British race (*M.a.yarrellii*) in having much
paler, grey upperparts. **VOICE** Call a
disyllabic 'tizzick'. Song a simple twittering,
incorporating flight call with frequent
pauses. **NEST** In hole or cavity in building,
wall or other man-made object.

★ **Grey Wagtail** *Motacilla cinerea*

| S | S | A | W | BUILDINGS, FARM, FRESH, MOOR, MOUNTAIN

Common resident and partial migrant. **ID** Graceful, long-tailed wagtail, a typical bird of fast-flowing streams and rivers. Yellow most intense on upper breast and undertail coverts; legs brownish-pink (all other wagtails' legs are black). Male brighter. Clear white central wing bar visible from above and below in flight. While perched or walking, constantly pumps tail up and down. **VOICE** Flight call more metallic than Pied Wagtail, a sharp 'tzi, tzi'. Song a series of flight calls strung together. **NEST** By waterside, in crevice of bank, amongst roots of tree or in hole in wall, bridge or other building.

male breeding

★★★ **Water Pipit** *Anthus spinoletta*

| S | S | A | W | COAST, FRESH, MARSH

Rare winter visitor from S Europe. **ID** In breeding plumage has grey head and pinkish tinge to breast, when can be confused with Scandinavian race of Rock Pipit (*A.p.littoralis*). In winter very similar to Rock Pipit but paler underparts, whiter 'eyebrow', white wing bars and white outer tail feathers. Unlike Rock Pipit, favours inland wetland sites, especially watercress beds. **VOICE** Flight call a single, thin 'tseep', compared with short run of notes given by Meadow Pipit.

breeding

★★ **Dartford Warbler** *Sylvia undata*

| S | S | A | W | HEATH

Fairly common but very localised resident. **ID** Elusive and skulking. A generally dark bird, grey above and dull wine-red below, brighter in male; long, graduated tail, usually cocked. Rapid, whirring flight on short wings. Usually found amongst gorse or heather. Often associates with Stonechat. **VOICE** A Wren-like scolding churr and rattle. Song a musical chatter recalling Whitethroat. **NEST** In scrub near ground.

male

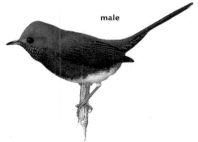

★ **Blackcap** *Sylvia atricapilla*

male

| S | S | **A** | **W** | FARM, GARDEN, WOOD

Very common summer visitor and scarce winter visitor
from Central Europe. **ID** Male is a grey bird with a black
cap. Both sexes lack white in tail. Female browner with
brown cap. Blackcaps breeding in Britain and Ireland
winter around W Mediterranean. **VOICE** Call a hard 'tac,
tac', louder than Lesser Whitethroat. Song a rich, fluty
warble, more varied but less sustained than Garden
Warbler. **NEST** Above ground in low bush, brambles,
evergreen or other woody vegetation.

★★★ **Barred Warbler**
Sylvia nisoria

| S | S | **A** | W | COAST, SCRUB

Rare autumn passage migrant from E Europe.
ID A large, heavy warbler with a heavy bill and
longish tail. Very rare in spring, when male is
heavily barred and has yellow iris. Autumn
birds are almost invariably immatures and have
buff fringes to upperwing coverts and tertials,
but show just a suggestion of barring on flanks
and undertail coverts. **VOICE** Call a harsh
'chack', sometimes repeated as a rattle.

male

★ **Bullfinch** *Pyrrhula pyrrhula*

| S | S | **A** | **W** | FARM, GARDEN, SCRUB, WOOD

Very common resident. **ID** Retiring habits, presence often
betrayed by the flash of a white rump as it flies away.
Plump, rounded breast and bull neck. Female greyish-
buff below. Pairs remain together throughout the year.
VOICE Haunting, piping 'hoee' contact call. Weak, creaky
song rarely heard. **NEST** In bush or shrub.

male

★ **Wheatear** *Oenanthe oenanthe*

| S | S | A | W | COAST, FARM, HEATH, MOOR, MOUNTAIN

Common summer visitor and fairly common passage migrant from Iceland and Greenland. **ID** Readily identified on ground by upright stance and white rump, especially visible as bird flies away. Female has plain brownish upperparts and no black mask. Restless, constantly on move, bobbing or fanning tail. **VOICE** Call a hard 'check', although often silent on migration. Song brief, explosive and rapid. **NEST** In hole in rocky crevice, stone wall or rabbit burrow.

breeding male

male

★ **Redstart** *Phoenicurus phoenicurus*

| S | S | A | W | PARK, SCRUB, WOOD

Common summer visitor; fairly common passage migrant from Scandinavia, mainly in autumn. **ID** Slim with upright stance. Chestnut tail constantly quivered. Female brown above and buff below. Rarely seen on ground. **VOICE** Call an anxious 'wee-tik-tik' and thin 'wheet'. Short song sweet, if slightly hoarse, rather like a Robin's with a terminal twitter. **NEST** In hole, generally in tree, but occasionally in wall or shed.

★★ **Black Redstart** *Phoenicurus ochruros*

| S | S | A | W | BUILDINGS, COAST

Rare breeder; scarce winter visitor and passage migrant from Europe. **ID** Often very elusive. Constantly quivering bright chestnut tail. Male greyish-black with white wing patch. Usually seen perched on building or fence from where it drops to feed briefly on ground. **VOICE** Scolding 'tucc-tucc' and snappy 'fist'. Short, loud, warbling song with terminal flourish. **NEST** In recess or hole in building, at sites such as power stations, gas works, railway sheds or derelict industrial areas.

female

male

male

★ **Whitethroat** *Sylvia communis*

`S | S | A | W` FARM, HEATH, SCRUB

Very common summer visitor. **ID** As name implies, has distinct white throat, particularly noticeable in singing or displaying male; broad chestnut area on closed wing; straw-coloured legs; tail often cocked. Female buff below. A restless bird, darting in and out of cover. **VOICE** Hoarse, scolding 'tchair'. Song an oft-repeated, brief, scratchy chattering, given during dancing song flight or from top of bush. **NEST** In low shrub or tall plants, e.g. nettles, about 30cm off ground.

★ **Lesser Whitethroat**
Sylvia curruca

`S | S | A | W` FARM, PARK, SCRUB

Common summer visitor and fairly common passage migrant. **ID** Smaller and more skulking than Whitethroat, with greyish-brown upperparts, dark cheek and dark grey legs. **VOICE** Call a single 'tick'. Song a preliminary subdued, brief warble followed by a boring rattle on a single note. **NEST** Low down in a bush or conifer.

male

★ **Linnet** *Carduelis cannabina*

`S | S | A | W` FARM, HEATH, SCRUB

Very common resident and partial migrant. **ID** Brown upperparts, warmer chestnut in male; primaries edged white, creating a diffuse, ill-defined, pale wing panel in flight. Female streaky brown, lacking pink on breast. Flocks in winter and spring. **VOICE** Flight call a rapid twittering. Song a rather quiet, musical twittering delivered from the top of a bush. **NEST** In thick bush, often gorse, and frequently in loose colony.

male breeding

★ **House Sparrow** *Passer domesticus*

| S | S | A | W | BUILDINGS, FARM, GARDEN

Abundant but declining resident. **ID** Rather dumpy brown and grey bird with a stout bill. Female lacks distinct head markings and is duller above. **VOICE** Various chirping calls that are strung together as an apology for a song. **NEST** In hole or crevice in a building, or a domed structure in creepers growing up a wall and occasionally in a bush or hedge.

★ **Dunnock** *Prunella modularis*

| S | S | A | W | FARM, GARDEN, SCRUB, WOOD

Abundant resident and fairly common passage migrant from N Europe. **ID** Sparrow-like bird with thin, warbler-like bill. At first glance, apparently dark and featureless, but closer inspection reveals a slate-grey head and breast. Shuffles around flicking its wings, rarely far from cover. A nervous bird that appears to be afraid of its own shadow! **VOICE** Call a thin, squeaky 'tew'. Song a fairly brief weak jingle, often given from the top of a bush. **NEST** In bush, hedge, evergreen or other area of cover.

★★★ **Wryneck** *Jynx torquilla* >

| S | S | A | W | COAST, PARK, SCRUB, WOOD

Rare breeding summer visitor and passage migrant from W Europe. **ID** Longish, rounded, barred tail, more obvious in flight. Vermiculated grey and brown upperparts with a black line along length of back; buffish breast; barred flanks. Crown feathers erected if alarmed; able to turn head almost 360 degrees. Undulating flight, when it recalls Red-backed Shrike or Barred Warbler. **VOICE** Alarm call a series of 'kee, kee, kee' notes, not unlike Lesser Spotted Woodpecker or distant raptor. **NEST** In hole or cavity in tree, wall or building.

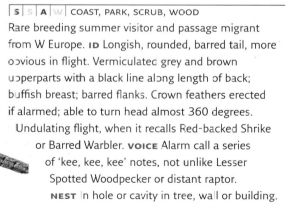

male

★★ **Marsh Harrier** *Circus aeruginosus*

| S | S | A | W | FARM, MARSH, REEDS

Scarce but increasing resident and summer visitor. **ID** Narrower wings and longer tail than Common Buzzard, but broader wings than other harriers. Male has contrasting grey, brown and black wings; female more uniform brown with pale, cream-coloured head and pale leading edge to inner wing. Rather lazy, low, quartering flight; also soars high in air with wings raised in shallow V. **NEST** On platform of dead vegetation in reedbed or on ground amongst cereal or arable crops.

★★ **Hen Harrier** *Circus cyaneus*

| S | S | A | W | COAST, FARM, HEATH, MARSH, MOOR, REED

Scarce resident, partial migrant and winter visitor from W Europe. **ID** A medium-sized raptor with long wings and tail. Smaller and slimmer winged than Marsh Harrier, but larger and broader winged than Montagu's Harrier. Male can appear almost white in flight. Male smaller than female, which is brown with a white rump known as a 'ring tail'. Low, buoyant flight with wings raised in a shallow V. **NEST** On ground in moorland, usually in shelter of taller vegetation.

male

★★★ **Montagu's Harrier** *Circus pygargus*

| S | S | A | W | FARM

Rare summer visitor; one of our rarest breeding birds. **ID** Smaller than Marsh and Hen Harriers with comparatively longer, narrower wings and long, narrow tail. Male has more extensive black on primaries and dark bars across underwing compared with male Hen Harrier. Female brown above with a white rump, known as a 'ring tail'. Buoyant, almost tern-like flight, especially male. **NEST** On ground, nowadays almost invariably amongst crops.

male

★★ Goshawk
Accipiter gentilis   m < f

| S | S | A | W | FARM, HEATH, WOOD

Scarce resident. **ID** Powerful, broad-winged, long-tailed raptor. Broad, white 'eyebrow'; both sexes barred grey below but male bluer above. In flight resembles a very large Sparrowhawk but has a distinct bulge at rear of inner wing, tail has broader base with more rounded tail corners and white undertail coverts are more obvious. Slower, more powerful wing beats; wings often look pointed when soaring. **NEST** In tree.

★ Sparrowhawk *Accipiter nisus*

| S | S | A | W | FARM, GARDEN, MARSH, PARK, WOOD

Common resident; fairly common winter visitor, mainly from Scandinavia. **ID** Nowadays almost as common as Kestrel. Long, thin, yellow legs visible when perched. Male smaller than female with orange barring on underparts. In flight, short, rounded wings and longish, barred, square-cornered tail. Infrequently perches out in open. **VOICE** Loud and rapid 'kek, kek, kek'. **NEST** At variable height in tree, sometimes in an old nest of another species.

male

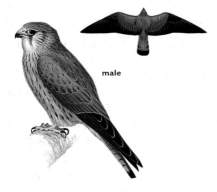

male

★★ **Merlin** *Falco columbarius*

| S | S | A | W | COAST, FARM, HEATH, MARSH, MOOR

Fairly common but localised breeder and partial migrant. **ID** The small, dashing falcon of open country that recalls a miniature Peregrine. Indistinct stripe below the eye. Female brownish-grey above, paler below; broadly barred tail. In flight rapid wing beats and occasional glides. **VOICE** Rapid 'ki-ki-ki-ki'. **NEST** Usually on ground in open moorland.

★★ **Peregrine** *Falco peregrinus*

| S | S | A | W | BUILDINGS, COAST, FARM, MOOR, MOUNTAIN

Fairly common but localised resident and partial migrant. **ID** Powerful, heavy-bodied falcon. In flight, pointed but fairly broad wings and shortish tail. Shallow wing beats with intermittent glides, but flies fairly rapidly and makes spectacular stoops at flying prey. **NEST** On cliff ledge or rocky outcrop, sometimes on ledge of building.

★★ **Hobby** *Falco subbuteo*

| S | S | A | W | FARM, FRESH, HEATH, MOOR

Scarce summer visitor. **ID** Contrasting white throat and black stripe below the eye; chestnut feathering on thighs and undertail coverts. In flight long, pointed, swept-back wings. Dashing, Swift-like flight enables it to take birds and insects in the air. **NEST** In tree in the nest of another larger bird or on a squirrel drey.

male

★ **Kestrel** *Falco tinnunculus*

| S | S | A | W | FARM, HEATH, MOOR, PARK, WOOD

Common resident and partial migrant.
ID Generally the most familiar bird of prey, readily identified by its hovering flight. Reddish-brown above with darker flight feathers. Male has blue-grey head and tail, female brown head and tail, barred darker. In flight, long, pointed wings and tail; only occasionally glides but frequently hovers with tail spread. Often seen perched on tree or telegraph pole. **VOICE** Shrill 'kee, kee, kee'. **NEST** On ledge or in a cavity of a cliff, building or tree.

★ **Cuckoo** *Cuculus canorus*

| S | S | A | W | FARM, HEATH, PARK, REEDS, WOOD

Common summer visitor. **ID** Slim with pointed wings and long, rounded tail, giving impression of a small falcon or Sparrowhawk. Yellow orbital ring, legs and feet. Rare female colour form brown above. Wings often held drooped at rest and in flight do not rise above the horizontal. **VOICE** Male gives the familiar 'cuckoo', female a bubbling trill. **NEST** Eggs laid in other birds' nests, parasitising particularly Dunnock, Meadow Pipit and Reed Warbler, the species chosen matching that in which the female Cuckook herself was reared.

male

male

★★★ **Great Grey Shrike**
Lanius excubitor

| S | S | A | W | HEATH, SCRUB

Rare winter visitor and passage migrant from N Europe.
ID The largest shrike to visit Britain and Ireland. Grey above, white below, with black mask and white patch on black wing; long, rounded tail. Perches on top of bushes and other exposed sites, but on occasion can be surprisingly elusive. Low, undulating flight and often hovers. **VOICE** Call a shrill trill, not unlike a Magpie.

★★★ **Crane** *Grus grus*

| S | S | A | W | FARM, MARSH, REEDS

Rare resident in E Anglia and passage migrant from Scandinavia and W Europe. **ID** Very large, with long legs and long, thin neck. Curved, drooping, blackish secondaries give appearance of a bushy tail. A shy bird, but spectacular duetting, dancing display in spring. In flight, neck and legs extended, slow, deep wing beats with groups flying in V formation; also soars. **VOICE** A far-carrying trumpeting. **NEST** A mound of vegetation on slightly raised, boggy ground.

★ **Grey Heron** *Ardea cinerea*

| S | S | A | W | COAST, FRESH, MARSH, REEDS, WOOD

Common resident and partial migrant; scarce winter visitor from NW Europe. **ID** Large grey heron with long legs, long neck and dagger-shaped, yellowish bill. Neck often retracted while standing. In flight neck retracted, dark flight feathers contrast with pale grey back and wing coverts; white 'headlights' in middle of leading edge of wings. **VOICE** Loud 'frank', often given in flight. **NEST** In colonies, nest often at top of tall tree.

★★★ **Purple Heron** *Ardea purpurea*

| S | S | A | W | FRESH, MARSH, REEDS

Rare passage migrant from W Europe, mainly in spring. **ID** Slightly smaller, more slender and darker than Grey Heron, with a more sinuous, serpentine neck, especially visible in flight when it hangs down well below level of body. Longer, narrower bill than Grey Heron. Dull wine-red underparts. In flight more bulging neck, less contrast in wing than Grey Heron, and legs and large feet extend further beyond tail. **VOICE** Higher pitched and less strident than Grey Heron.

★★ **Water Rail** *Rallus aquaticus*

S S A W FRESH, MARSH, REEDS

Fairly common resident and winter visitor. **ID** An elusive bird of the reedbeds that is more often heard than seen, especially in summer. Laterally compressed body perfectly adapted for slipping between reed stems, as are long toes for walking on mud or floating vegetation. Barred flanks; white undertail coverts. Weak flight with dangling legs; also swims short distances. **VOICE** A variety of groans and grunts (called sharming), the most common a pig-like squeal, given especially at night. **NEST** On or near ground level in tall vegetation growing in or near water.

★ **Grey Partridge** *Perdix perdix*

S S A W FARM

Very common but declining resident **ID** Rotund, chicken-like bird with small head and very short neck. Smaller than Red-legged Partridge; both species have reddish tail. Male more brightly marked with larger belly patch. Flies low with whirring wing beats and short, stiff-winged glides. **VOICE** When flushed an excited 'krri, krri, krri'. Song rather hoarse 'kieerric', with accent on last syllable. **NEST** On ground in tall grass, vegetation or crop.

male

★★ **Ptarmigan** *Lagopus mutus*

S S A W MOUNTAIN

Fairly common but very localised resident of Scottish mountains. **ID** A typical grouse with white wings and belly at all seasons. In summer, female barred buffy-brown where male is grey; in winter both sexes all white except for black tail. **VOICE** A low, harsh, belch-like croak. **NEST** On ground in shelter of rock or patch of vegetation.

male
summer

139

★ **Dunlin** *Calidris alpina*

`S` `S` `A` `W` COAST, MARSH, MOOR, MOUNTAIN

Fairly common, mainly upland breeder; very common
coastal passage migrant and winter visitor from
Greenland, Iceland and N Europe. **ID** The most
abundant shore wader in winter, often found in large
flocks. Length of bill varies according to sex and race,
with longest billed breeding in Arctic. In summer
chestnut on back and black belly. **VOICE** Flight call
a rolling 'treee'. **NEST** On ground in grassy tussock.

non-breeding

non-breeding

★ **Sanderling** *Calidris alba*

`S` `S` `A` `W` COAST

Fairly common winter visitor from Siberia to
sandy coasts. **ID** Small, strikingly white wader
in winter, characteristic of open sandy beaches;
rather short, stout bill. In breeding plumage,
rufous upper breast sharply demarcated from
white underparts. In flight, distinct white wing
bars. Runs back and forth following the ebb
and flow of the waves. **VOICE** Flight call a
liquid 'quit-quit'.

★★ **Little Stint** *Calidris minuta*

`S` `S` `A` `W` COAST, MARSH

Scarce passage migrant, mainly in autumn, from
Arctic Norway and Siberia; rare but regular in winter.
ID Smallest of the common waders and often found in
flocks with Dunlin. Dainty; pale V on back; short,
straight bill; legs black. In breeding plumage has
chestnut tinge to head, upper breast and back.
More rapid feeding action than Dunlin. **VOICE** Shrill,
high-pitched 'tit'.

non-breeding

★★ **Curlew Sandpiper**
Calidris ferruginea

| S | S | A | W | MARSH

Scarce visitor from Arctic Siberia, mainly to coastal marshes in autumn. **ID** Slightly larger, longer necked and more upright than Dunlin, with longer, more decurved bill and longer legs. In summer, brick-red head and underparts. **VOICE** Flight call a very distinctive, liquid 'chirrip'.

non-breeding

★★★ **Red-necked Phalarope**
Phalaropus lobatus

<

| S | S | A | W | COAST, FRESH, MARSH

Rare summer visitor to N Isles; elsewhere scarce passage migrant to coasts and inland pools. **ID** Smaller and daintier than Grey Phalarope with very fine, all-black bill. Very rarely seen in winter plumage in Europe. Unmistakable in breeding plumage, with yellow stripes on back and red on nape and upper breast. Often very tame and feeds by pecking rapidly from side to side while spinning on surface of water. During breeding season, female more brightly coloured than male. **NEST** In poolside tussock.

★★★ **Grey Phalarope**
Phalaropus fulicarius

<

| S | S | A | W | COAST, MARSH

Uncommon visitor from Arctic to coastal waters or pools, usually after strong gales. **ID** Thicker billed than Red-necked Phalarope, with yellowish tinge at base. Very rarely seen in Britain and Ireland in breeding plumage, when has deep chestnut neck and underparts. Usually very tame and feeds by pecking rapidly from side to side while spinning on surface of water. During breeding season, female more brightly coloured than male.

non-breeding

★ **Grey Plover**
Pluvialis squatarola

| S | s | A | W | COAST

Fairly common passage migrant and winter
visitor from W Siberia. **ID** A rather stout,
hunchbacked plover with a heavy bill, rarely
found inland or on freshwater marshes. Male in
breeding plumage has blacker underparts.
In flight, white rump and black 'armpits'. Slow
and deliberate feeding action. **VOICE** Flight call
a plaintive, trisyllabic 'tlee, oo, ee'.

breeding

non-breeding

★ **Knot** *Calidris canutus*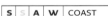

| S | s | A | **W** | COAST

Very common but localised winter visitor from the
Arctic, mainly to the larger estuaries. **ID** A dumpy wader,
larger and stockier than Dunlin; rather short, thickish
straight bill; shortish legs. In breeding plumage, has
chestnut head and underparts. In flight, pale grey rump.
Forms massive, dense, roosting flocks at high tide; when
disturbed, birds fly in close formation, creating a smoke-
like effect. **VOICE** Flight call a disyllabic 'kwip, kwip'.

non-breeding

★★ **Purple Sandpiper**
Calidris maritima

| S | s | **A** | **W** | COAST

Rare breeder in Scotland and fairly common
but localised winter visitor from Norway and
the Arctic. **ID** A rather dumpy, dull slaty-grey
wader with short, orange-ish legs and base to
bill. In breeding plumage, has scaly, chestnut
and whitish upperparts. In flight, very dark
upperparts. Feeds on rocky coasts often in
mixed flocks with Turnstones. **VOICE** A short
'trit, trit'.

non-breeding

★★ Greenshank
Tringa nebularia

| S | S | A | W | COAST, FRESH, MARSH, MOOR

Scarce resident, moving south and west in autumn; also autumn passage migrant from NE Europe. **ID** Larger than Redshank with longer, slightly upturned bill and greenish legs. In flight, extensive white wedge up back. **VOICE** Flight call a ringing, shrill, trisyllabic 'tew, tew, tew'. **NEST** On ground on moorland, often near a log or dead branch and not far from water.

non-breeding

breeding

★★ Spotted Redshank
Tringa erythropus

non-breeding

| S | S | A | W | FRESH, MARSH

Scarce passage migrant and winter visitor from Fennoscandia. **ID** Elegant, slim wader with long, fine bill and long legs All black in breeding plumage, except for white wedge on rump and lower back. Will wade in deeper water, when it feeds by swimming and upending. **VOICE** Flight call a disyllabic 'chewit'.

★★ Black-tailed Godwit
Limosa limosa

| S | S | A | W | COAST, MARSH

Rare breeder in England; fairly common winter visitor from Iceland. **ID** Large, elegant wader with long bill and legs. Orange head, neck and breast in breeding plumage. In flight, broad white wing bars and white rump. Often found in large flocks outside breeding season. **VOICE** Lapwing-like flight call and oft-repeated 'wicka-wicka-wicka...' in display flight. **NEST** On ground in lush vegetation on grassy meadow or marshland.

non-breeding

★★ **Glaucous Gull** *Larus hyperboreus* >

| S | S | **A** | **W** | COAST

Scarce winter visitor from the Arctic, mainly to coasts. **ID** Slightly smaller than Great Black-backed Gull, but appears heavier; aggressive appearance due to sloping forehead with peak at rear of crown and large bill; closed wing barely extends beyond tail. Adult appears white-winged in flight with broad wings. **VOICE** Similar to Herring Gull.

★★ **Iceland Gull** *Larus glaucoides*

| **S** | S | A | **W** | COAST

Scarce winter visitor from the Arctic, mainly to coasts of Scotland and Ireland, occasionally inland. **ID** Smaller and gentler looking than Glaucous Gull. About size of Herring Gull, but rather slim, attenuated shape; rounded head with peak above eye; whitish primaries; pink legs at all ages. Adult appears white-winged in flight, but with slimmer wings than Glaucous Gull. **VOICE** Similar to Herring Gull.

non-breeding

★ **Herring Gull** *Larus argentatus*

| **S** | **S** | **A** | **W** | COAST, FARM

Very common resident around much of the coastline, spreading inland in winter; common winter visitor from N Europe. **ID** The common gull around much of the British and Irish coast. Large size and pink legs at all ages. First winter fairly uniformly brown, becoming paler in second year. Aggressive disposition, even on occasion towards humans. **VOICE** The familiar cry around many of our harbours. **NEST** On cliff ledges, in sand dunes or increasingly on flat-topped buildings near the sea.

non-breeding

breeding

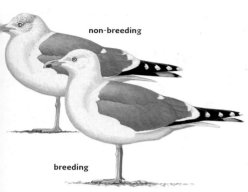

non-breeding

breeding

★★ Yellow-legged Gull
Larus michahellis

| S | S | **A** | **W** | COAST, MARSH |

Scarce autumn and winter visitor. **ID** Very similar to Herring Gull and only recently classified as a separate species. Compared with Herring Gull, adult has slightly darker upperparts, whiter head with minimal streaking and yellow legs. In flight, adult has more black and smaller white spots on wing tips than Herring Gull.

★ Lesser Black-backed Gull
Larus fuscus

| **S** | **S** | **A** | **W** | COAST, FARM, FRESH |

Common summer visitor to coastal and inland colonies; more widespread, especially inland, in winter. **ID** Smaller and less barrel-chested than Great Black-backed Gull with smaller, less angular bill. Immature dark greyish-brown with grey upperparts appearing from second year onwards. **VOICE** Deeper, more nasal call than Herring Gull. **NEST** On ground on grassy coastal slopes or in sand dunes.

non-breeding

★ Fulmar *Fulmarus glacialis*

| **S** | **S** | **A** | **W** | COAST |

Very common breeder on coastal cliffs, resident apart from a couple of months in early autumn when moulting at sea; abundant in selected coastal waters in winter. **ID** Superficial resemblance to gulls, but lacks dark wing tips; bull neck and short, thick, tube-nose bill. Buoyant on water; takes off by pattering along surface. Effortless gliding flight on stiff wings with only occasional wing beats. Breeding ledges occupied even during winter. Dark form (known as Blue Fulmar) dark grey above and below, commonest in Arctic. **VOICE** Raucous cackling calls on ledges. **NEST** On bare cliff ledge or grassy outcrop.

★ Common Gull *Larus canus*

| **S** | **S** | **A** | **W** | COAST, FARM, FRESH, MOOR

Common breeder around inland and coastal waters in Scotland and Ireland; elsewhere very common winter visitor from N and Central Europe, except in upland and moorland areas. **ID** Recalls smaller version of Herring Gull, with more rounded head and less heavy bill. First-winter brownish wings, pink base to bill and pink legs. Also known as Mew Gull. **VOICE** High-pitched, laughing calls. **NEST** On ground, usually in colonies.

★★★ Ring-billed Gull
Larus delawarensi

| **S** | **S** | **A** | **W** | COAST, FRESH

Rare winter visitor from N America, mainly to SW coasts. **ID** Between Common and Herring Gulls in size and bulk. Adult has paler grey upperparts than other similar gulls and broad black band across bill. Immature plumages very similar to Common Gull of same age. In flight, adult has very little white on wing tip. Generally a restless bird, rarely remaining still for any length of time.

★ Black-headed Gull
Chroicocephalus ridibundus

| **S** | **S** | **A** | **W** | COAST, FARM, FRESH

Very common breeder around inland and coastal waters; abundant winter visitor from N Europe to most areas except the uplands. **ID** The commonest and most familiar inland gull, also the smallest of the common gulls. Black spot behind eye replaces dark hood in winter. Immature has brown bars across upperwings and black tip to tail. The only common gull to have a white leading edge on the outer wing. Readily takes scraps from garden lawns. **NEST** On open ground, often in large colonies.

★★ Mediterranean Gull
Larus melanocephalus

| S | S | A | W | COAST |

Rare localised breeder, usually in Black-headed Gull colonies; elsewhere scarce winter visitor from Central Europe, but becoming more numerous. **ID** Slightly larger than Black-headed Gull with stouter bill and longer legs. Black smudge behind eye in winter at all ages. In flight, adult appears white-winged. **VOICE** Distinctive, almost cat-like 'mee-ow'. **NEST** On ground in gull colony.

non-breeding

breeding

non-breeding

breeding

★ Kittiwake *Rissa tridactyla*

| S | S | A | W | COAST |

Very common summer visitor to coastal cliffs; generally scarce in coastal waters in winter. **ID** An elegant gull with a buoyant flight; dark legs and feet. In flight adult has all-black wing tip, immature has a black W across the wings. **VOICE** Cries out its name, 'kittiwake', mainly around colonies. **NEST** On ledges of precipitous sea cliffs or coastal buildings.

★★ Little Gull
Hydrocoloeus minutus

| S | S | A | W | COAST |

Scarce winter visitor and passage migrant from NE Europe to coastal waters, occasionally inland. **ID** Our smallest and daintiest gull. Black spot behind eye and darkish cap replace hood in winter. In flight wing tips appear rounded and adult is white-winged above, but has distinctly dark underwing; immature has a black W across the wings recalling immature Kittiwake. Feeds by dipping tern-like to snatch food from surface of water.

non-breeding

breeding

★ **Arctic Tern** *Sterna paradisaea*

| S | S | A | W | COAST

Common summer visitor to coastal colonies, mainly in Scotland and Ireland. **ID** Slightly smaller and daintier than Common Tern, with shorter neck and bill and longer tail streamers; bill entirely blood red in breeding plumage; very short legs. In flight, underwing has neat black line along trailing edge of outer feathers on otherwise pure white primaries. Sometimes takes food from surface of water like Black Tern. **VOICE** A drawn-out 'prree-ah'. **NEST** In colony on sand, shingle or grass near the coast.

breeding

★ **Common Tern** *Sterna hirundo*

| S | S | A | W | COAST, FRESH

Common and widely dispersed summer visitor to colonies bordering coast and on inland waters. **ID** Pure white underparts; black-tipped red bill is longer than in Arctic Tern. In flight, dark wedge on outer upperwing and fairly broad, ill-defined, dark trailing edge to primaries on underwing. Hovers and dives for food. **VOICE** Noisy and quarrelsome, a series of 'kierri-kierri-kierri'. **NEST** On ground in colony on sand or shingle bank, or on islands on freshwater lakes.

breeding

★★★ **Roseate Tern** *Sterna dougallii*

| S | S | A | W | COAST

Rare summer visitor to a small number of well-scattered colonies. **ID** The most elegant and beautiful of the breeding terns. Size of Common Tern but with paler upperwing recalling small Sandwich Tern, a longer, darker bill and very long tail streamers. In breeding plumage has pink flush on breast and dark red base to bill. In flight, wings white apart from a narrow black wedge along leading edge of primaries. Dives powerfully into water to feed. **VOICE** Distinctly disyllabic 'tchivik', likened to flight call of Spotted Redshank. **NEST** On ground in coastal colony, often amongst other species of terns.

breeding

breeding

★ Sandwich Tern
Sterna sandvicensis

| S | S | A | W | COAST

Common but localised summer visitor to scattered coastal colonies. **ID** Large tern with a long, thin, black bill with a yellow tip, shaggy crest and short tail. In flight, appears whiter than other terns. Feeds by flying along with bill pointing down, before closing wings and diving rapidly into water like a miniature Gannet. **VOICE** Distinctive grating 'kerrick'. **NEST** On sand or shingle banks in large colonies.

★★ Little Tern *Sternula albifrons*

| S | S | A | W | COAST

Fairly common summer visitor to coastal colonies. **ID** Very small, noisy tern with rapid wing beats. Hovers just above water surface before diving to catch fish. **VOICE** Oft-repeated, rasping, chattering calls. **NEST** In colonies on sandy or shingle beaches.

breeding

non-breeding

★★ Black Tern *Chlidonias niger*

| S | S | A | W | COAST, FRESH

Scarce or in some years fairly common visitor to both inland and coastal waters, mainly in spring. **ID** Smaller, shorter winged and less rakish than Common Tern. In breeding plumage, has all black head and underparts. Feeds by dipping down to water surface; does not dive.

★★ **Barnacle Goose**
Branta leucopsis

| s | s | A | **W** | FARM, MARSH |

Localised winter visitor from Arctic, mainly to
Scotland and Ireland; scattered feral populations
elsewhere. **ID** Silvery-grey barred upperparts;
completely white face, sometimes tinged
yellowish. Often feeds in large flocks in winter.
VOICE At a distance, a flock recalls the sound
of a pack of yapping dogs.

★ **Brent Goose**
Branta bernicla

| **s** | s | **A** | **W** | COAST, FARM, MARSH |

Very common winter visitor from Siberia
and Greenland, mainly to S and E coasts
and Ireland. **ID** Smallest goose, about size
of Mallard; generally dark appearance; white
collar visible at close range. In winter grazes in
large, closely packed flocks, often with Wigeon.
VOICE Distinctive chattering, guttural calls.

★ **Pink-footed Goose**
Anser brachyrhynchus

| s | s | **A** | **W** | COAST, FARM, MARSH |

Very common winter visitor from Arctic
to scattered traditional sites. **ID** Small goose,
short dark neck and dark head; pink legs and
small black bill with pink band. Many have
blue-grey tinge to upperparts. In flight, short
neck and dark head, pale upperwing and back.
In winter often occurs in vast flocks, but
individuals remain in family groups within
flock. **VOICE** Rather harsh, high-pitched ringing
calls, best remembered as 'pink, pink'.

★★★ Snow Goose
Anser caerulescens

dark form

| S | S | A | **W** | FARM, MARSH |

Rare visitor from N America, but feral birds
not infrequently occur. **ID** Adult white form
entirely white apart from black primaries;
adult dark form (known as Blue Goose)
mainly dark with white restricted to head,
upper neck and tip of tail. **VOICE** An unusual
soft cackling.

★★ Bewick's Swan *Cygnus columbianus*

| S | S | A | **W** | FARM, FRESH, MARSH |

immature

Fairly common winter visitor from Siberia to scattered, often traditional
locations, mainly in S and W. **ID** Smallest and daintiest of our three swans,
with comparatively short, straight neck; a smaller version of Whooper Swan.
Immature plumage paler, greyer and more uniform than immature Mute
Swan. Adult white with small, rounded yellow area at
base of largely black bill. Migrates and winters in
family groups. **VOICE** Higher pitched and more
yelping than Whooper Swan, with notes given singly
or at most in twos.

★★ Whooper Swan *Cygnus cygnus*

| S | S | A | **W** | FARM, FRESH, MARSH |

Rare breeder in Scotland; fairly common winter visitor
from N Europe and Iceland to many traditional sites,
mainly in N and W. **ID** Larger than Bewick's Swan,
neck appears longer and straighter than Mute Swan.
Immature paler, greyer and more uniform than
immature Mute Swan, with long, wedge-shaped bill
yellowish at base and pink near tip. Adult plumage
entirely white with largely yellow bill. Migrates and
winters in family groups. **VOICE** The most vocal swan,
with loud, bugling calls, often given in groups of 3-4.

immature

★★ Smew *Mergellus albellus*

female

`S` `S` `A` `W` FRESH

Scarce winter visitor from NE Europe and Siberia to inland waters. **ID** Female small and compact, known as 'red heads'. Adult drake very distinctive, mainly white. Feeds by diving. Lone birds are often rather shy, tending to feed near aquatic vegetation among which they can readily hide.

★ Goosander *Mergus merganser*

`S` `S` `A` `W` FRESH

Fairly common breeder on rivers and inland waters in N and W, spreading further south in winter. **ID** Large, long, heavy body; long red bill with hooked tip. Female has distinct crest and sharp division between chestnut head and grey neck. Drake has dark green head and white underparts with a pink flush in winter. Feeds by diving, often in groups. **NEST** In hole in tree, bank or amongst boulders near water.

female

★ Red-breasted Merganser *Mergus serrator*

female

`S` `S` `A` `W` COAST, FRESH

Fairly common breeder in freshwater and tidal habitats in N and W, moving to coastal waters in winter. **ID** Smaller and slimmer than Goosander; shaggy crest; finer bill. In female, chestnut of head 'merges' into grey neck. Drake has dark green head and brown breast. **NEST** Concealed under vegetation or boulders near water.

male

★★ Goldeneye *Bucephala clangula*

`S` `S` `A` `W` COAST, FRESH

Rare localised breeder inland in Scotland; fairly common winter visitor from Scandinavia to both coastal and inland waters. **ID** Large, rounded head with peaked crown; small bill and yellow iris; white panel often visible on closed wing. Drake has glossy green head with white patch at base of bill, white breast and flanks. Dives frequently when feeding. **NEST** In hole in tree.

female

★ **Pochard** *Aythya ferina*

| S | S | A | W | FRESH

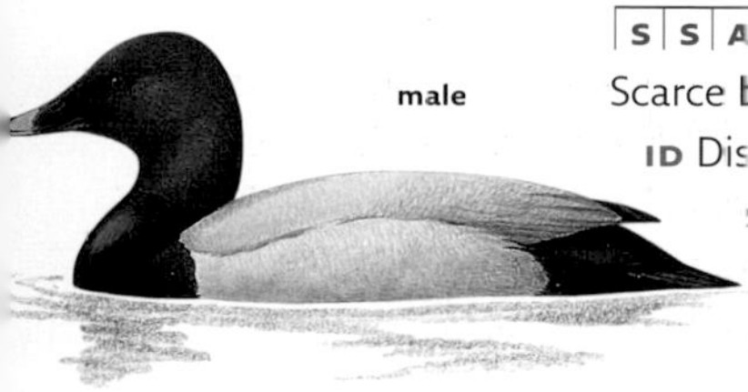

male

Scarce breeder; common winter visitor from Central Europe.
ID Distinctive peaked crown and sloping forehead forming
sweeping curve along top of bill, which in drake has
grey band. Female fairly uniform pale grey-brown.
Gregarious diving duck, rarely found alone.
NEST Pile of plant material in waterside vegetation.

★ **Wigeon** *Anas penelope*

| S | S | A | W | FRESH, MARSH

Scarce breeder mainly in N; very common winter visitor
from N Europe and Siberia. **ID** Adult drake shows yellow
central crown stripe and white wing patch in flight.
Female has variable chestnut underparts. Grazing
ducks often form large winter flocks and join
Brent Geese on coastal saltings and marshes.
VOICE Drake gives characteristic drawn-out
whistle. **NEST** On ground in thick waterside
vegetation.

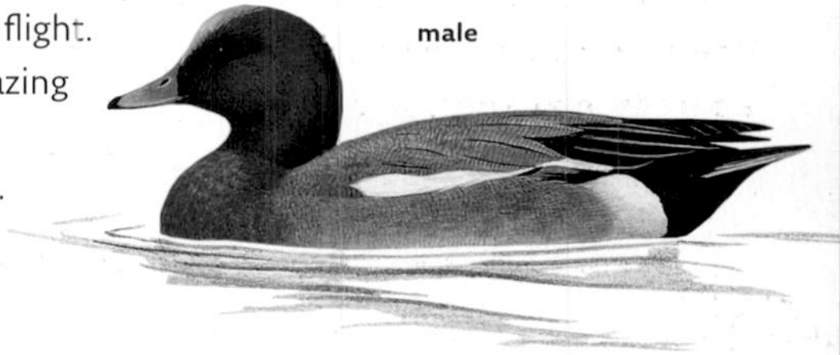

male

★★ **Mandarin** *Aix galericulata*

| S | S | A | W | FRESH, PARK, WOOD

Scarce resident feral population mainly in S. **ID** Breeding
plumage of drake the most spectacular and unmistakable of
any British duck, with orange fans on face and orange 'sails'
on back. Female has grey head. Green panel may be
visible on closed wing of female. In flight, streamlined shape and uniformly dark upperwings.
NEST In hole in tree.

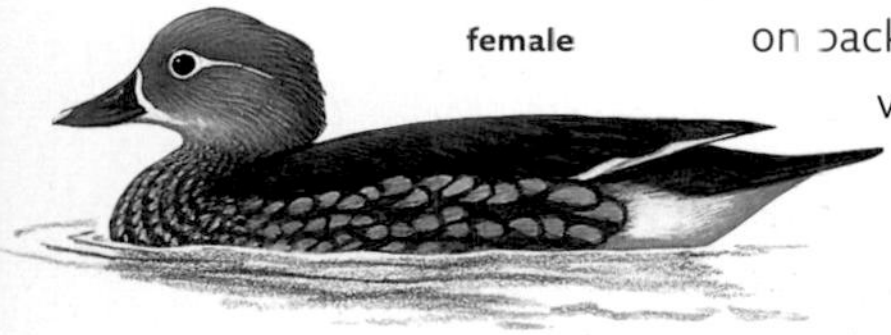

female

★ **Scaup** *Aythya marila*

| S | S | **A** | **W** | COAST |

Fairly common winter visitor, mainly from Iceland, to estuarine and coastal waters. **ID** Marine equivalent of Tufted Duck; rounded head, yellow eye and grey bill. Female dull brown with paler flank. In flight, drake black and white.

male

★★ **Garganey** *Anas querquedula*

| S | S | A | W | FRESH |

Scarce summer visitor to scattered localities. **ID** Small, slightly built dabbling duck; size of Teal but bill longer. Female all brown with pale 'eyebrow' and spot at base of bill. Feeds by dipping head or skimming surface; unobtrusive and easily overlooked. **VOICE** Crackling display call. **NEST** Concealed in long grass or rushes near water.

male

★ **Teal** *Anas crecca*

| S | S | **A** | **W** | FRESH, MARSH |

Fairly common breeder in N and W; very common winter visitor from N Europe and Siberia. **ID** Our smallest duck. Drake has horizontal white stripe along flank and yellow triangle on rear flank. Female all brown. Feeds by upending and leaps from water on taking off, hence the collective noun a 'spring' of Teal. **VOICE** Very vocal when displaying in groups, giving a high-pitched, chirruping call. **NEST** Well concealed in ground vegetation.

male

★ **Gadwall** *Anas strepera*

| S | S | A | W | FRESH

Scarce breeder mainly in S; fairly common in winter. **ID** White panel often visible on closed wing. Female all brown and very similar to female Mallard, but head greyer, lower mandible brighter orange and lacks white sides to tail. Surface feeder, frequently in small groups. **VOICE** Drake gives dry, croaking call not unlike Mallard. **NEST** On ground in thick vegetation near water.

male

★ **Mallard** *Anas platyrhynchos*

| S | S | A | W | FARM, FRESH, MARSH

Very common resident; winter visitor from Scandinavia and Iceland. **ID** The familiar duck of urban parks; yellow bill and orange legs. Only adult drake has iridescent green head. Female all brown. Feeds by dabbling on surface and upending. **VOICE** Typical duck's quacking. **NEST** Usually well concealed amongst ground vegetation.

male

★ **Pintail** *Anas acuta*

| S | S | A | W | FRESH, MARSH

Rare breeder at scattered localities; common winter visitor from N Europe and Siberia mainly to the larger estuaries. **ID** Slim and elegant compared with other wildfowl. Female all brown with uniform buff-coloured head and grey bill. Feeds by upending. **NEST** Amongst low vegetation near water.

male

★★ Black-throated Diver
Gavia arctica

| S | S | A | W | COAST, FRESH

Scarce breeder in Scotland; fairly common winter visitor to selected coastal waters. **ID** Intermediate between Red-throated and Great Northern Divers in size and shape; dagger-like bill held horizontally. In breeding plumage, front of neck black with extensive white markings on upperparts. **NEST** Shallow scrape on mound, usually on small island.

non-breeding

breeding

non-breeding

breeding

★ Red-throated Diver
Gavia stellata

| S | S | A | W | COAST, FRESH

Fairly common but localised breeder in Scotland; common winter visitor to coastal waters. **ID** Commonest, smallest and slimmest diver; bill uptilted and held pointing skywards. In breeding plumage, dull wine-red patch on front of neck and uniform brown upperparts. **NEST** Shallow scrape on mound by shore.

★★ Great Northern Diver
Gavia immer

| S | S | A | W | COAST

Fairly common winter visitor from Iceland and Nearctic to coastal waters, mainly off Scotland and Ireland. **ID** Largest of the three divers; angular head shape with peaked forecrown and thick neck; heavy, dagger-like bill held horizontally. In breeding plumage, entirely black head with striped white patch on side of neck and extensive white markings on upperparts.

non-breeding

★★★ Grey Phalarope
Phalaropus fulicarius

| S | S | **A** | **W** | COAST, MARSH

Uncommon visitor from Arctic to coastal waters or pools, usually after strong gales. **ID** Thicker billed than Red-necked Phalarope, with yellowish tinge at base. In flight recalls Sanderling. Usually very tame and feeds by pecking rapidly from side to side while spinning on surface of water. During breeding season, female more brightly coloured than male.

non-breeding

★★★ Red-necked Phalarope
Phalaropus lobatus

| **S** | **S** | **A** | W | COAST, FRESH, MARSH

Rare summer visitor to N Isles; elsewhere scarce passage migrant to coasts and inland pools. **ID** Smaller and daintier than Grey Phalarope with very fine, all-black bill. Unmistakable in breeding plumage. Very rarely seen in winter plumage in Europe. Often very tame and feeds by pecking rapidly from side to side while spinning on surface of water. During breeding season, female more brightly coloured than male. **NEST** In poolside tussock.

non-breeding

female

male

★ **Chaffinch** *Fringilla coelebs*

| S | S | A | W | FARM, GARDEN, HEATH, PARK, WOOD

Abundant resident and winter visitor, mainly from Scandinavia. **ID** One of our most widespread birds and the second commonest. Male has blue head and pinkish-chestnut underparts. In flight, double white wing bars and white sides to tail. In winter, sexes often found in separate flocks. **VOICE** Cheerful 'spink' and a difficult to locate 'hooeet'. Song a vigorous cascade with a terminal flourish, tirelessly repeated after a short interval and often followed by a nearby rival's song. **NEST** In fork of tree or bush.

★★ **Pied Flycatcher** *Ficedula hypoleuca*

| S | S | A | W | COAST, WOOD

Fairly common but localised summer visitor; fairly common autumn passage migrant from Scandinavia. **ID** Both sexes have white wing flashes and white sides to tail. Male black above, white below. A very active small flycatcher that is rarely still; even when perched it has the habit of flicking its tail and one wing. **VOICE** Call a frequently repeated 'whit' or anxious 'phweet'. An uninspiring song consisting of a repetition of two notes with an occasional trill. **NEST** In hole in tree or in a nest box.

male

female

male

★★ **Hawfinch** *Coccothraustes coccothraustes* >

| S | S | A | W | PARK, WOOD

Fairly common but localised resident. **ID** Large finch with a very powerful, heavy bill. Strange, club-shaped extensions on inner primaries. In flight, broad white wing bars visible on upper and underside of wings; broad white tip to tail. Often found in vicinity of hornbeams. Very wary and despite flocking in winter can be extremely elusive. **VOICE** A Robin-like 'tzic'. **NEST** On horizontal branch of tree at varying height, often in loose colony of a few pairs.

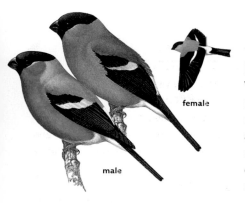

★ **Bullfinch** *Pyrrhula pyrrhula*

| S | S | A | W | FARM, GARDEN, SCRUB, WOOD

Very common resident. **ID** Retiring habits, presence often betrayed by the flash of a white rump as it flies away. Plump, rounded breast and bull neck. Male bright reddish-pink on underparts. **VOICE** Haunting, piping 'hoee' contact call. Weak, creaky song rarely heard. **NEST** In bush or shrub.

female

male

★★ **Snow Bunting** *Plectrophenax nivalis*

| S | S | A | W | COAST, MOUNTAIN

Rare breeder in Scotland; fairly common winter visitor from Greenland, Iceland and Scandinavia. **ID** Male in breeding plumage unmistakable; in winter, both sexes have streaked, buff upperparts and white underparts; male has extensive white patches on inner wings. Feeds in flocks in winter on beaches and coastal fields, resembling drifting snowflakes in flight. **VOICE** Flight call 'prrritt, teu', recalling Little Ringed Plover. Song a brief but musical twitter, often given in flight. **NEST** On ground amongst rocks or boulders.

female

male breeding

male non-breeding

★★★ **Hoopoe**
Upupa epops

| S | S | A | W | FARM, GARDEN, HEATH, PARK

Rare passage migrant from Europe. **ID** Unmistakable, pinkish-buff bird with black and white bars across wings; long, erectile black and white crest; long, thin, decurved bill. Broadly rounded wings with characteristic undulating, floppy flight. Feeds on ground, often on areas of short grass. **VOICE** Far-carrying, hollow-sounding 'poo, poo, poo'.

★ Pied Wagtail
Motacilla yarrellii

| S | S | A | W | BUILDINGS, FARM, GARDEN, MARSH

Very common resident and partial migrant. **ID** Our only small black and white bird with a long tail that is constantly wagged up and down. Adult male has black upperparts; both sexes have blackish rump. Breeding in the rest of Europe is the race *M.a.alba* (White Wagtail), which is a scarce visitor to Britain and Ireland, and differs from the British race (*M.a.yarrellii*) in having much paler, grey upperparts. **VOICE** Call a disyllabic 'tizzick'. Song a simple twittering incorporating flight call with frequent pauses. **NEST** In hole or cavity in building, wall or other man-made object.

male breeding
Pied Wagtail

female
Pied Wagtail

male
White Wagtail

★ Grey Wagtail
Motacilla cinerea

| S | S | A | W | BUILDINGS, FARM, FRESH, MOOR, MOUNTAIN

Common resident and partial migrant. **ID** Graceful, long-tailed wagtail, a typical bird of fast-flowing streams and rivers. Yellow most intense on upper breast and undertail coverts; legs brownish-pink (all other wagtails' legs are black). Male brighter. Clear white central wing bar visible from above and below in flight. While perched or walking, constantly pumps tail up and down. **VOICE** Flight call more metallic than Pied Wagtail, a sharp 'tzi, tzi'. Song a series of flight calls strung together. **NEST** By waterside, in crevice of bank, amongst roots of tree or in hole in wall, bridge or other building.

male breeding

★★★ Great Grey Shrike *Lanius excubitor*

| S | S | **A** | **W** | HEATH, SCRUB

Rare winter visitor and passage migrant from N Europe. **ID** The largest shrike to visit Britain and Ireland. Grey above, white below, with black mask and white patch on black wing; long, rounded tail. Perches on top of bushes and other exposed sites, but on occasion can be surprisingly elusive. Low, undulating flight and often hovers. **VOICE** Call a shrill trill, not unlike a Magpie.

male

★ Wood Pigeon
Columba palumbus

| **S** | **S** | **A** | **W** | FARM, GARDEN, SCRUB, WOOD

Abundant resident. **ID** Our largest and bulkiest dove. White patch on sides of neck and white bar across wing in flight. Explodes noisily from cover when disturbed; display flight involves loud wing claps and glides. Highly gregarious at most times of the year. **VOICE** A five-syllable cooing with a gap between the second and third notes. May be remembered as 'I'm a... Wood Pigeon'. **NEST** In tree, bush or hedge.

★★ Black Grouse *Tetrao tetrix*

| S | **S** | A | **W** | FARM, HEATH, MOOR, WOOD

Localised and declining resident. **ID** Female brown, barred darker, some with notched tail. Males gather into communal display groups, called 'leks', in spring. Male also known as Blackcock and female as Greyhen. **VOICE** Male gives bubbling calls, audible at long range. **NEST** On ground amongst low plants.

male

161

★ **Wheatear** *Oenanthe oenanthe*

| S | S | A | W | COAST, FARM, HEATH, MOOR, MOUNTAIN

Common summer visitor and fairly common passage migrant from Iceland and Greenland. **ID** Readily identified on ground by upright stance and white rump, especially visible as bird flies away. Female has plain brownish upperparts and no black mask. In flight, much of tail and rump white. Restless, constantly on move, bobbing or fanning tail. Greenland and Iceland race (*O.o.leucorhoa*) larger, more boldly marked and with a tendency to perch on bushes. **VOICE** Call a hard 'check', although often silent on migration. Song brief, explosive and rapid. **NEST** In hole in rocky crevice, stone wall or rabbit burrow.

female

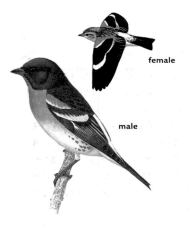

female

male

★★ **Brambling** *Fringilla montifringilla*

| S | S | A | W | FARM, GARDEN, WOOD

Occasional breeder in Scotland; common winter visitor, mainly from Fennoscandia. **ID** Size and shape of Chaffinch. In all plumages has orange tinge to the breast. Flight silhouette recalls shape of flying fish; white rump less obvious in female. Associates with Chaffinches; often found feeding on beech mast in winter. **VOICE** Loud, harsh, questioning 'tchweep' and quiet 'tchup'.

★ **Bullfinch** *Pyrrhula pyrrhula*

| S | S | A | W | FARM, GARDEN, SCRUB, WOOD

Very common resident. **ID** Retiring habits, presence often betrayed by the flash of a white rump as it flies away. Female greyish-buff below. In flight, distinct white rump. **VOICE** Haunting, piping 'hoee' contact call. Weak, creaky song rarely heard. **NEST** In bush or shrub.

female

male

★★ **Snow Bunting** *Plectropherax nivalis*

| S | s | **A** | **W** | COAST, MOUNTAIN

Rare breeder in Scotland; fairly common winter visitor
from Greenland, Iceland and Scandinavia. **ID** Male in
breeding plumage unmistakable; in winter, both sexes
have streaked, buff upperparts and white underparts;
male has extensive white patches on inner wings. n
flight, both sexes show white rump. Single birds often
very tame, but flocks restless and unapproachable.
Typically feeds in flocks in winter on beaches and
coastal fields, resembling drifting snowflakes in flight.
VOICE Flight call 'prrritt, teu', recalling Little Ringec
Plover. Song a brief but musical twitter, often given in
flight. **NEST** On ground amongst rocks or boulders.

male breeding

female breeding

★ **Goldfinch** *Carduelis carduelis*

| S | S | **A** | **W** | FARM, GARDEN, PARK, SCRUB, WOOD

Very common and increasing resident and partial
migrant. **ID** Sexes very similar, but male a little
brighter with more extensive red on face. In flight,
shows indistinct white rump. Feeds on thistles and
teasels. **VOICE** Cheerful, trisyllabic flight call 'swit,
wit, wit'. Song a mixture of rapid trills and twitters,
incorporating the flight call. **NEST** In crown of tree,
often on thinner, outer branch.

★ **Jay** *Garrulus glandarius*

`S` `S` `A` `W` FARM, GARDEN, PARK, WOOD

Very common resident. **ID** Bright blue wing patch finely barred black. In flight, distinct white rump. Raises crown feathers in alarm or display. Often moves around in small, noisy parties. **VOICE** Loud and raucous 'tchaar'. A great mimic; song comprises a bizarre mixture of clicks, mews and chuckles. **NEST** In fork against main trunk of tree.

★★★ **Hoopoe** *Upupa epops*

`S` `S` `A` `W` FARM, GARDEN, HEATH, PARK

Rare passage migrant from Europe. **ID** Unmistakable, pinkish-buff bird. In flight, broadly rounded wings with characteristic undulating, floppy flight, black and white bars across wings and a white rump. Feeds on ground, often on areas of short grass. **VOICE** Far-carrying, hollow-sounding 'poo, poc, poo'.

★★ **Rock Dove** *Columba livia*

`S` `S` `A` `W` BUILDINGS, COAST, FARM

A fairly common resident of coastal cliffs in N and W Britain and Ireland. **ID** Paler grey above than Stock Dove, with double black wing bar and white rump; also white underwing. Feral Pigeon generally lacks white rump, but present in some individuals. **VOICE** Familiar cooing. **NEST** Tend to be colonial with nests in caves or crevices in sea cliffs.

★ **House Martin** *Delichon urbicum*

`S` `S` `A` `W` BUILDINGS, COAST

Very common summer visitor. **ID** Short, forked tail with no streamers. In flight, appears black above with distinct white rump. Glides more than Swallow. **VOICE** A chirruping twitter in flight; shrill alarm call. **NEST** Usually in colony, enclosed mud nest with entrance hole near top, built under eaves or locally on cliffs.

★★★ **White-tailed Eagle** *Haliaeetus albicilla*   >

| S | S | A | W | COAST

Rare resident and winter visitor from N Europe. **ID** Very large eagle with broad, parallel-sided wings, large head with massive bill and shortish, wedge-shaped tail. Adult has white tail. Shallow, relaxed wing beats with only the occasional glide. Catches fish with talons from surface of water. **NEST** In tree top or on cliff face or rocky pinnacle.

★★★ **Rough-legged Buzzard**
Buteo lagopus

| S | S | A | W | FARM, HEATH, PARK

Rare winter visitor from Scandinavia. **ID** Larger and longer winged than Common Buzzard. Underparts very pale with dark belly and white tail with broad, dark terminal band. Distinct black mid-wing patches also visible from below in flight. Frequently hovers on slowly beating wings.

★★ **Hen Harrier** *Circus cyaneus*

| S | S | A | W | COAST, FARM, HEATH, MARSH, MOOR, REED

Scarce resident, partial migrant and winter visitor from W Europe. **ID** Medium-sized raptor with long wings and tail. Smaller and slimmer winged than Marsh Harrier, but larger and broader winged than Montagu's Harrier. Adult male pale grey and black. In flight, female brown with a white rump. Low, buoyant flight with wings raised in a shallow V. **NEST** On ground in moorland, usually in shelter of taller vegetation.

female

★★★ **Montagu's Harrier** *Circus pygargus*

| S | S | A | W | FARM

Rare summer visitor; one of our rarest breeding birds. **ID** Smaller than Marsh and Hen Harriers with comparatively longer, narrower wings and long, narrow tail. Adult male pale grey and black. In flight, female brown with a white rump. Buoyant, almost tern-like flight, especially in male. **NEST** On ground, nowadays almost invariably amongst crops.

female

★ **Barn Owl** *Tyto alba*

| S | S | A | W | BUILDINGS, COAST, FARM, PARK, SCRUB

Fairly common resident. **ID** The palest of our owls, with a distinctive heart-shaped face; may appear ghostly white. Nocturnal and crepuscular. In flight, shows a rather lazy flight action, but turns suddenly on spotting potential prey, when may hover or drop to ground. **VOICE** Distinctive blood-curdling shriek and a shrill squeal. **NEST** In hole in tree, building, rocky crevice or nestbox.

★★ **Snow Bunting** *Plectrophenax nivalis*

| S | S | A | W | COAST, MOUNTAIN

Rare breeder in Scotland; fairly common winter visitor from Greenland, Iceland and Scandinavia. **ID** Male in breeding plumage unmistakable; in winter, both sexes have streaked, buff upperparts and white underparts; male has extensive white patches on inner wings. Typically feeds in flocks in winter on beaches and coastal fields, resembling drifting snowflakes in flight. **VOICE** Flight call 'prrritt, teu', recalling Little Ringed Plover. Song a brief but musical twitter, often given in flight. **NEST** On ground amongst rocks or boulders.

male breeding

★★ **Ptarmigan**
Lagopus mutus

| S | S | A | W | MOUNTAIN

Fairly common but very localised resident of Scottish mountains. **ID** A typical grouse with white wings and belly at all seasons, but during summer head, breast and back grey in male, brown in female. **VOICE** A low, harsh, belch-like croak. **NEST** On ground in shelter of rock or patch of vegetation.

male winter

breeding

★★★ **Spoonbill** *Platalea leucorodia*

| S | S | A | W | FRESH, MARSH

Rare summer visitor; has bred in England. **ID** Large, all-white wading bird; long bill with spoon-shaped tip; long, drooping crest and ochre breast band present only in breeding plumage. In flight, both neck and legs extended; groups fly in line astern. **NEST** In trees and reedbeds.

★★★ **White Stork** *Ciconia ciconia*

| S | S | A | W | FARM, FRESH, MARSH

Rare summer visitor from Europe, mainly in spring and early summer. Many records refer to escapes from captivity or the re-introduction programme in the Netherlands. **ID** Unmistakable large black and white bird with long red bill and legs. In flight, both neck and legs extended; soars on thermals to gain height.

★★ **Little Egret** *Egretta garzetta*

| S | S | A | W | COAST, FRESH, MARSH, WOOD

Scarce but increasing resident; first bred in Britain and Ireland in 1996. **ID** In last few years has become a familiar bird on many coastal marshes in S and E England. Medium-sized, all-white heron; bill slim and black; yellow feet conspicuous in flight. Long, fine, drooping head plume in breeding plumage. In flight, neck tucked in and legs extended. **NEST** In colonies in trees and bushes.

breeding

167

★ **Oystercatcher** *Haematopus ostralegus* >

| S | S | A | W | COAST, FARM, FRESH

Common resident, partial migrant and winter visitor, mainly from Iceland and Norway. **ID** One of our most familiar coastal waders, now spreading inland. Distinctive pied plumage and long, stout, orange-red bill. Very noisy both in flight and on ground. **VOICE** Shrill 'peep', repeated many times during piping display in pairs or small groups. **NEST** On beach, dunes, arable and grassy land or amongst rocks.

non-breeding

★★ **Black-tailed Godwit**
Limosa limosa >

| S | S | A | W | COAST, MARSH

Rare breeder in England; fairly common winter visitor from Iceland. **ID** Large, elegant wader. Lacks orange head, neck and breast in winter. In flight, distinct white wing bars and white rump patch. Often found in large flocks outside breeding season. **VOICE** Lapwing-like flight call and oft-repeated 'wicka-wicka-wicka...' in display flight. **NEST** On ground in lush vegetation on grassy meadow or marshland.

★ **Redshank** *Tringa totanus* <

| S | S | A | W | COAST, FRESH, MARSH, MOOR

Common but declining breeder and winter visitor, mainly from Iceland. **ID** The noisy wader of marshland. In flight, shows broad white trailing edge to wing, and white rump extending up lower back. Bobs when alarmed. **VOICE** Call when agitated and in flight a loud, ringing 'tleu, leu, leu'. Song given in flight a musical version of the flight call repeated many times. **NEST** On ground in grassy tussock.

non-breeding

★★ **Stone Curlew** *Burhinus oedicnemus*

`S` `S` `A` `W` FARM, HEATH

Scarce summer visitor. **ID** Large, ungainly bird with a rather hunched appearance. Large yellow eyes an adaptation to its nocturnal habits. In flight, bold black and white wing pattern. Walks or runs rather furtively with body held horizontally, trying to avoid detection. Extremely well camouflaged when standing still or sitting on ground. **VOICE** Loud, penetrating and eerie Curlew-like calls heard mainly at night during breeding season. **NEST** On bare ground.

★ **Turnstone** *Arenaria interpres*

non-breeding

`S` `S` `A` `W` COAST

Common winter visitor from the Arctic, mainly to rocky coasts. **ID** In flight, 'harlequin' pattern across wings and upperparts. In winter, dark above and white below. Searches for food by flipping over pebbles, seaweed, etc. **VOICE** Flight call a metallic, staccato 'tuk-a-tuk'.

★ **Grey Plover** *Pluvialis squatarola*

non-breeding

`S` `S` `A` `W` COAST

Fairly common passage migrant and winter visitor from W Siberia. **ID** Rather stout, hunchbacked wader, rarely found inland or on freshwater marshes. Black underparts in breeding plumage. In flight, white wing bars and rump, and black 'armpits'. Slow and deliberate feeding action. **VOICE** Flight call a plaintive, trisyllabic 'tlee, oo, ee'.

★ **Knot** *Calidris canutus*

non-breeding

`S` `S` `A` `W` COAST

Very common but localised winter visitor from the Arctic, mainly to the larger estuaries. **ID** Dumpy wader, larger and stockier than Dunlin. In breeding plumage, has chestnut head and underparts. In flight, white wing bars and pale grey rump. Forms massive, dense, roosting flocks at high tide; when disturbed birds fly in close formation, creating a smoke-like effect. **VOICE** Flight call a disyllabic 'kwip-kwip'.

★ Common Sandpiper
Actitis hypoleucos

| S | S | A | w | COAST, FRESH, MOOR

Common but localised summer visitor; rare in winter.
ID Attenuated shape and longish tail accentuated by
horizontal carriage; brown patches on either side of
breast separated from closed wing by 'tongue' of
white. In flight, shows distinct white wing bar. Flies
low over water. Constantly bobs tail end while walking
or resting. **VOICE** Flight call a run of 5–6 high-pitched,
piping notes 'twee-wee-wee-wee...'. Song a
rhythmically repeated series of similar calls. **NEST** On
open ground or amongst vegetation, close to water.

non-breeding

★ Ringed Plover
Charadrius hiaticula

| S | S | A | W | COAST, FARM, FRESH, HEATH

Fairly common resident and passage migrant from Canada,
Greenland, Iceland and Fennoscandia. **ID** One of the most
characteristic breeding birds of our coasts. Easily recognised
by broad black breast band; orange bill and legs. Long winged
in flight with prominent but narrow white wing bar. Butterfly-
like display flight while giving song. **VOICE** Flight call a
distinctive, soft, disyllabic 'too, lee'. Song a fairly rapid,
mellow series of trilling flight calls. **NEST** On ground on sand,
shingle or bare ground near water.

breeding

★ Sanderling *Calidris alba*

| S | S | A | W | COAST

Fairly common winter visitor from Siberia to sandy
coasts. **ID** Small, strikingly white wader in winter,
characteristic of open sandy beaches. In breeding
plumage, rufous upper breast sharply demarcated from
white underparts. In flight, very distinct, long, white wing
bar. Runs back and forth following ebb and flow of waves.
VOICE Flight call a liquid 'quit-quit'.

non-breeding

non-breeding

★★★ **Red-necked Phalarope**
Pnalaropus lobatus

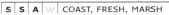

| S | S | A | W | COAST, FRESH, MARSH

Rare summer visitor to N Isles; elsewhere scarce passage migrant to coasts and inland pools. **ID** Smaller and daintier than Grey Phalarope. Very rarely seen in winter plumage in Europe. In flight, narrow white wing bar and striped back. Often very tame and feeds by pecking rapidly from side to side while spinning on surface of water. During breeding season, female more brightly coloured than male. **NEST** In poolside tussock.

★★★ **Grey Phalarope**
Phalaropus fulicarius

| S | S | A | W | COAST, MARSH

Uncommon visitor from Arctic to coastal waters or pools, usually after strong gales. **ID** Compared with Red-necked Phalarope bill, is thicker and has yellowish tinge at base. In flight recalls Sanderling, but wing bar restricted to inner wing. Usually very tame and feeds by pecking rapidly from side to side while spinning on surface of water. During breeding season, female more brightly coloured than male.

non-breeding

non-breeding

★ **Dunlin** *Calidris alpina*

| S | S | A | W | COAST, MARSH, MOOR, MOUNTAIN

Fairy common, mainly upland breeder; very common coastal passage migrant and winter visitor from Greenland, Iceland and N Europe. **ID** The most abundant shore wader in winter, often found in large flocks. In summer, chestnut on back and black belly; in winter, grey upperparts. In flight, narrow white wing bar. **VOICE** Flight call a rolling 'treee'. **NEST** On ground in grassy tussock.

★ **Oystercatcher** *Haematopus ostralegus*

| S | S | A | W | COAST, FARM, FRESH

Common resident, partial migrant and winter visitor, mainly from Iceland and Norway. **ID** One of our most familiar coastal waders, now spreading inland. Distinctive pied plumage and long, stout, orange-red bill. Very noisy both in flight and on ground. **VOICE** Shrill 'peep', repeated many times during piping display in pairs or small groups. **NEST** On beach, dunes, arable and grassy land or amongst rocks.

★ **Redshank** *Tringa totanus*

| S | S | A | W | COAST, FRESH, MARSH, MOOR

non-breeding

Common but declining breeder and winter visitor, mainly from Iceland. **ID** The noisy wader of marshland. In flight, shows broad white trailing edge to wing, and white rump extending up lower back. Bobs when alarmed. **VOICE** Call when agitated and in flight a loud, ringing 'tleu, leu, leu'. Song given in flight a musical version of the flight call repeated many times. **NEST** On ground in grassy tussock.

★★ **Spotted Redshank** *Tringa erythropus*

| S | S | A | W | FRESH, MARSH

Scarce passage migrant and winter visitor from Fennoscandia. **ID** Elegant, slim wader. All black (apart from white rump) in breeding plumage. In flight, white wedge along rump and lower back. Will wade in deeper water, where it feeds by swimming and upending. **VOICE** Flight call a disyllabic 'chewit'.

non-breeding

★★ **Greenshank** *Tringa nebularia*

| S | S | A | W | COAST, FRESH, MARSH, MOOR

Scarce resident, moving south and west in autumn; also autumn passage migrant from NE Europe. **ID** Larger than Redshank, with longer, slightly upturned bill and greenish legs. In flight, extensive white wedge on tail, rump and lower back. **VOICE** Flight call a ringing, shrill trisyllabic 'tew, tew, tew'. **NEST** On ground on moorland, often near a log or dead branch, and not far from water.

non-breeding

★ **Curlew** *Numenius arquata*

S | S | A | W COAST, FARM, HEATH, MARSH, MOOR

Common but localised breeder and winter visitor to
the coast from N Europe. **ID** Our largest wader, with a
very long, decurved bill. In flight, white rump
extends to lower back; bill is equal to or longer
than width of inner wing. Flies in lines or
chevrons with slow, rather deliberate wing
beats. **VOICE** Call given on taking off and in flight
'courlooeee', with an upward inflection at end. Song
a liquid, rhythmic, bubbling trill. **NEST** On ground
amongst heather or other low vegetation.

★★ **Whimbrel**
Numenius phaeopus

S | S | A | W COAST, FARM, MOOR

Scarce summer visitor to Scotland; fairly common
passage migrant from N Europe. **ID** Smaller cousin
of the Curlew, with a shorter, less decurved bill. In
flight, darker, more contrasting upperparts than
Curlew, bill shorter than width of inner wing and
more rapid wing beats. **VOICE** A rapid, tittering trill
of seven whistles given in flight. Song a bubbling
trill recalling Curlew. **NEST** On ground in the open.

★ **Bar-tailed Godwit** *Limosa lapponica*

S | S | A | W COAST

Common winter visitor from Arctic Russia and Siberia
to flat coastal areas. **ID** Appears smaller than Black-
tailed Godwit due to shorter legs; bill long and
slightly upcurved. Plain chestnut underparts in
summer. In flight, pattern of upperparts recalls
Whimbrel or Curlew. **VOICE** Flight call a sharp
'keewick'.

non-breeding

★★ **Curlew Sandpiper**
Calidris ferruginea < 🐦

non-breeding

| S | S | A | W | MARSH |

Scarce visitor from Arctic Siberia, mainly to coastal
marshes in autumn. **ID** Slightly larger and longer winged
than Dunlin. In winter, grey above and white below.
In flight, narrow white wing bar and white rump.
VOICE Flight call a very distinctive, liquid 'chirrip'.

non-breeding

★★ **Wood Sandpiper** *Tringa glareola* < 🐦

| S | S | A | W | FRESH, MARSH |

Rare summer visitor to Scotland; scarce passage migrant
mainly in autumn from N Europe. **ID** Recalls Green
Sandpiper but has paler brown upperparts with more
speckling, a distinct white 'eyebrow' and longer, yellowish
legs. In flight, less contrasting upperparts than Green
Sandpiper and pale underwing. **VOICE** Flight call a distinct
'chiff, chiff, chiff'. **NEST** Usually on ground, occasionally
in shrub or tree.

★★ **Green Sandpiper** *Tringa ochropus* < 🐦

| S | S | A | W | FRESH, MARSH |

Fairly common passage migrant and scarce winter visitor
from N Europe; has bred occasionally. **ID** Very dark brown,
almost black upperparts and breast contrasting with
white below. In flight, looks like an outsize House Martin
with a prominent, square, white rump and dark
underwing. A rather shy wader, easily flushed; bobs like a
Common Sandpiper. **VOICE** In flight, gives a clear, ringing
'tluee, wee, wee' with an upward inflection at the start.
NEST Usually on the ground.

non-breeding

non-breeding

★ Grey Plover
Pluvialis squatarola

| s | s | A | W | COAST

Fairly common passage migrant and winter visitor from W Siber a. **ID** Rather stout, hunchbacked wader, rarely found inland or on freshwater marshes Lacks black underparts in winter. In flight, white wing bars and rump, black 'armpits'. Slow and deliberate feeding action. **VOICE** Flight call a plaintive, trisyllabic 'tlee, oo, ee'.

★★ Black-tailed Godwit
Limosa limosa

| s | s | A | W | COAST, MARSH

Rare breeder in England; fairly common winter visitor from Iceland to southern estuaries. **ID** Large, elegant wader. Orange head, neck and breast in breeding plumage. In flight, distinct white wing bars and white rump. Outside breeding season often found in large flocks. **VOICE** Lapwing-like flight call and oft-repeated 'wicka-wicka-wicka...' in display flight. **NEST** On ground in lush vegetation on grassy meadow or marshland.

non-breeding

★ Lapwing *Vanellus vanellus*

| s | s | A | W | COAST, FARM, MARSH

Very common but decreasing lowland breeder; abundant winter visitor from N Europe. **ID** One of the characteristic birds of farmland. Appears black and white, but upperparts have greeny-purple iridescence. In flight, black wings contrast with white wing tips and rump. Tumbling display flight in spring. Often in large flocks out of breeding season. Also known as Peewit or Green Plover. **VOICE** Scolding 'peewee'. **NEST** On ground on field or marshland.

★ **Gannet** *Morus bassanus*

breeding | S | S | A | W | COAST

Very common breeder in a few scattered colonies around N and W coasts; elsewhere fairly common in coastal waters, especially in autumn. **ID** Large black and white or brown seabird with heavy, dagger-like bill. Adult has ochre flush on head in breeding plumage. When feeding, dives steeply into sea with wings closed just before entry into water, bobbing back to surface like a cork. **NEST** In gannetries on ground or rocky ledge.

★★ **Glaucous Gull** *Larus hyperboreus*

| s | s | A | W | COAST

Scarce winter visitor from the Arctic, mainly to coasts. **ID** Slightly smaller than Great Black-backed Gull, but appears heavier; aggressive appearance due to sloping forehead with peak at rear of crown and large bill. Adult appears white-winged in flight with broad wings. **VOICE** Similar to Herring Gull.

non-breeding

★★ **Iceland Gull** *Larus glaucoides*

non-breeding

| S | s | A | W | COAST

Scarce winter visitor from the Arctic, mainly to coasts of Scotland and Ireland, occasionally inland. **ID** Smaller and gentler looking than Glaucous Gull. About size of Herring Gull, but rather slim, attenuated shape; comparatively long wings, which when closed extend well beyond tail. Appears white-winged in flight, but with slimmer wings than Glaucous Gull. **VOICE** Similar to Herring Gull.

★ **Herring Gull** *Larus argentatus*

| S | S | A | W | COAST, FARM

Very common resident around much of the coastline, spreading inland in winter; common winter visitor from N Europe. **ID** The common gull around much of the British and Irish coast. Large size and pink legs at all ages. Aggressive disposition, even on occasion towards humans. **VOICE** The familiar cry around many of our harbours. **NEST** On cliff ledges, in sand dunes or increasingly on flat-topped buildings near the sea.

non-breeding

breeding

non-breeding

breeding

★★ Yellow-legged Gull
Larus michahellis

| s | s | **A** | **W** | COAST, MARSH

Scarce autumn and winter visitor. **ID** Very similar to Herring Gull and only recently classified as a separate species. Compared with Herring Gull, adult has slightly darker upperparts, whiter head with minimal streaking and yellow legs. In flight, adult has more black and smaller white spots on wing tips than Herring Gull.

★ Great Black-backed Gull
Larus marinus

| **s** | **s** | **A** | **W** | COAST, FARM

Common coastal resident in N and W. and joined in E by winter visitors from N Europe. **ID** Largest, most maritime of British breeding gulls. More barrel chested than Lesser Black-backed Gull, with very heavy, deep, angular bill; pink legs at all ages. **VOICE** Deeper and gruffer than Herring Gull. **NEST** On top of rock stacks or islands.

breeding

★ Lesser Black-backed Gull
Larus fuscus

non-breeding

| **s** | **s** | **A** | **W** | COAST, FARM, FRESH

Common summer visitor to coastal and inland colonies; more widespread, especially inland, in winter. **ID** Smaller and less barrel-chested than Great Black-backed Gull with smaller, less angular bill. **VOICE** Deeper, more nasal call than Herring Gull. **NEST** On ground on grassy coastal slopes or in sand dunes.

★ Fulmar *Fulmarus glacialis*

| **s** | **s** | **A** | **W** | COAST

Very common breeder on coastal cliffs, resident apart from a couple of months in early autumn when moulting at sea; abundant in selected coastal waters in winter. **ID** Superficial resemblance to gulls but lacks dark wing tips; bull neck and short, thick, tube-nose bill. Effortless gliding flight on stiff wings with occasional wing beats. **VOICE** Raucous cackling calls. **NEST** On bare cliff ledge or grassy outcrop.

★ **Common Gull** *Larus canus*

| s | s | A | w | COAST, FARM, FRESH, MOOR

Common breeder around inland and coastal waters in Scotland and Ireland; elsewhere very common winter visitor from N and Central Europe, except in upland and moorland areas. **ID** Recalls smaller version of Herring Gull, with more rounded head and less heavy bill. First-winter brownish wings, pink base to bill and pink legs. Also known as Mew Gull. **VOICE** High-pitched, laughing calls. **NEST** On ground, usually in colonies.

non-breeding

breeding

non-breeding

breeding

★★★ **Ring-billed Gull**
Larus delawarensis

| s | s | A | w | COAST, FRESH

Rare winter visitor from N America, mainly to SW coasts. **ID** Between Common and Herring Gulls in size and bulk. Adult has paler grey upperparts than other similar gulls and broad black band across bill. In flight, adult has very little white on wing tip. Generally a restless bird, rarely remaining still for any length of time.

★ **Black-headed Gull**
Chroicocephalus ridibundus

| s | s | A | w | COAST, FARM, FRESH

Very common breeder around inland and coastal waters; abundant winter visitor from N Europe to most areas except the uplands. **ID** The commonest and most familiar inland gull, also the smallest of the common gulls. Black spot behind eye replaces dark hood in winter. Immature has brown bars across upperwings and black tip to tail. The only common gull to have a white leading edge on the outer wing. Readily takes scraps from garden lawns. **NEST** On open ground, often in large colonies.

non-breeding

breeding

★★ Mediterranean Gull
Larus melanocephalus

| S | S | A | W | COAST |

Rare localised breeder, usually in Black-headed Gull colonies; elsewhere scarce winter visitor from Central Europe, but becoming more numerous. **ID** Slightly larger than Black-headed Gull with stouter bill and longer legs. Black smudge behind eye in winter at all ages. In flight, adult appears white-winged. **VOICE** Distinctive, almost cat-like 'mee-ow'. **NEST** On ground in gull colony.

non-breeding

breeding

non-breeding

breeding

★ Kittiwake *Rissa tridactyla*

| S | S | A | W | COAST |

Very common summer visitor to coastal cliffs; generally scarce in coastal waters in winter. **ID** An elegant gull with a buoyant flight; dark legs and feet. In flight adult has all-black wing tip, immature has a black W across the wings. **VOICE** Cries out its name, 'kittiwake', mainly around colonies. **NEST** On ledges of precipitous sea cliffs or coastal buildings.

★★ Little Gull
Hydrocoloeus minutus

| S | S | A | W | COAST |

Scarce winter visitor and passage migrant from NE Europe to coastal waters, occasionally inland. **ID** Our smallest and daintiest gull. Black spot behind eye and darkish cap replace hood in winter. In flight wing tips appear rounded and adult is white-winged above, but has distinctly dark underwing; immature has a black W across the wings recalling immature Kittiwake. Feeds by dipping tern-like to snatch food from surface of water.

non-breeding

breeding

★ **Arctic Tern** *Sterna paradisaea*

| S | S | A | W | COAST

Common summer visitor to coastal colonies, mainly in Scotland and Ireland. **ID** Slightly smaller and daintier than Common Tern, with shorter neck and bill and longer tail streamers; bill entirely blood red in breeding plumage; very short legs. In flight, underwing has neat black line along trailing edge of outer feathers on otherwise pure white primaries. Sometimes takes food from surface of water like Black Tern. **VOICE** A drawn-out 'prree-ah'. **NEST** In colony on sand, shingle or grass near the coast.

breeding

★ **Common Tern** *Sterna hirundo*

| S | S | A | W | COAST, FRESH

Common and widely dispersed summer visitor to colonies bordering coast and on inland waters. **ID** Pure white underparts; black-tipped red bill is longer than in Arctic Tern. In flight, dark wedge on outer upperwing and fairly broad, ill-defined, dark trailing edge to primaries on underwing. Hovers and dives for food. **VOICE** Noisy and quarrelsome, a series of 'kierri–kierri–kierri'. **NEST** On ground in colony on sand or shingle bank, or on islands on freshwater lakes.

breeding

★★★ **Roseate Tern** *Sterna dougallii*

| S | S | A | W | COAST

Rare summer visitor to a small number of well-scattered colonies. **ID** The most elegant and beautiful of the breeding terns. Size of Common Tern but with paler upperwing and very long tail streamers. In breeding plumage, has pink flush on breast and dark red base to bill. In flight, wings white apart from a narrow black wedge along leading edge of primaries. Dives powerfully into water to feed. **VOICE** Distinctly disyllabic 'tchivik', likened to flight call of Spotted Redshank. **NEST** On ground in coastal colony, often amongst other species of terns.

breeding

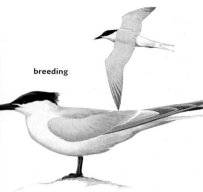

breeding

★ Sandwich Tern
Sterna sandvicensis

| S | S | A | W | COAST

Common but localised summer visitor to scattered coastal colonies. **ID** Large tern with a long, thin, black bill with a yellow tip, shaggy crest and short tail. In flight, appears whiter than other terns. Feeds by flying along with bill pointing down, before closing wings and diving rapidly into water like a miniature Gannet. **VOICE** Distinctive grating 'kerrick'. **NEST** On sand or shingle banks in large colonies.

★★ Little Tern *Sternula albifrons*

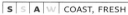

| S | S | A | W | COAST

Fairly common summer visitor to coastal colonies. **ID** Very small, noisy tern with rapid wing beats. Hovers just above water surface before diving to catch fish. **VOICE** Oft-repeated, rasping, chattering calls. **NEST** In colonies on sandy or shingle beaches.

breeding

non-breeding

★★ Black Tern *Chlidonias niger*

| S | S | A | W | COAST, FRESH

Scarce or in some years fairly common visitor to both inland and coastal waters, mainly in spring. **ID** Smaller, shorter winged and less rakish than Common Tern. In breeding plumage, has all black head and underparts. Feeds by dipping down to water surface; does not dive.

white form

★★★ Snow Goose
Anser caerulescens

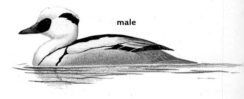

| S | S | A | **W** | FARM, MARSH |

Rare visitor from N America, but feral birds not infrequently occur. **ID** White form unmistakable. Dark form (known as Blue Goose) mainly dark with white restricted to head, upper neck and tip of tail. **VOICE** An unusual soft cackling.

★★ Smew *Mergellus albellus*   < 🦆

| S | S | A | **W** | FRESH |

Scarce winter visitor from NE Europe and Siberia to inland waters. **ID** Adult drake unmistakable. Female and immature drake grey with brown head, known as 'red heads'. In flight, adult drake black and white. Feeds by diving. Lone birds often shy, tending to feed near aquatic vegetation among which they can readily hide.

male

★★ Black Guillemot
Cepphus grille   < 🦅

| S | S | **A** | **W** | COAST |

Fairly common resident of rocky areas in Scotland and Ireland. **ID** Smaller than Guillemot, with shorter bill. Our only auk with a white head in winter. In breeding plumage, all black except for large white oval on closed wing; bright red legs and feet. Known as Tystie in Scotland. **NEST** In hole in base of cliff or under boulder.

non-breeding

★ **Mute Swan** *Cygnus olor*   >

| S | S | A | W | FARM, FRESH, MARSH

Common and widespread lowland resident. **ID** The familiar swan of our park lakes is the largest bird in Britain and Ireland; long neck held either straight or in a gentle curve. Feeds by upending; adopts a threatening posture with wings arched like sails and head lowered over back, known as 'busking'. **VOICE** Hissing noise when being aggressive. In flight, wings produce a pulsating sound. **NEST** High mound of reeds or other vegetation on or by water's edge.

female

male

★★ **Whooper Swan** *Cygnus cygnus*   >

| S | S | A | W | FARM, FRESH, MARSH

Rare breeder in Scotland; fairly common winter visitor from N Europe and Iceland to many traditional sites, mainly in N and W. **ID** Larger than Bewick's Swan, neck appears longer and straighter than Mute Swan. Long, wedge-shaped bill, mainly yellow and forming point with black tip. Not easy to separate from Bewick's Swan in flight. Migrates and winters in family groups. **VOICE** The most vocal swan, with loud, bugling calls, often given in groups of 3-4.

★★ **Bewick's Swan** *Cygnus columbianus*   >

| S | S | A | W | FARM, FRESH, MARSH

Fairly common winter visitor from Siberia to scattered, often traditional locations, mainly in S and W. **ID** Smallest and daintiest of our three swans, with comparatively short, straight neck; diagnostic bill pattern with yellow confined to base of bill; a smaller version of Whooper Swan. Not always easy to separate from Whooper Swan in flight. **VOICE** Higher pitched and more yelping than Whooper Swan, with notes given singly or at most in twos.

★ **Great Crested Grebe** *Podiceps cristatus*

| S | S | A | W | COAST, FRESH

Widespread resident of lowland waters. **ID** Largest, slimmest and most elegant grebe; long, slender neck and bill. Ornate head plumes in breeding plumage. Appears predominantly black and white in winter. In flight, shows more white on upperwing than Red-necked Grebe. Breeding pairs engage in head-turning displays. **NEST** On mound of aquatic vegetation near water's edge.

non-breeding

★★ **Red-necked Grebe**
Podiceps grisegena

| S | S | A | W | COAST, FRESH

Scarce winter visitor from NE Europe to coastal waters, mainly in S and E, with a few inland. **ID** Rarely seen in full breeding plumage in Britain and Ireland. In winter, shows dark cheek and some chestnut on neck. In flight, less white on upperwing than Great Crested Grebe. Leaps up before diving.

non-breeding

★★ **Slavonian Grebe** *Podiceps auritus*

| S | S | A | W | COAST, FRESH

Rare breeder, mainly in Scotland; scarce winter visitor to coastal waters. **ID** In breeding plumage, a most beautiful bird with golden tufts on top of head. In winter, black above and white below. In flight, has a small area of white on forewing. The most maritime of our grebes. **NEST** On floating mound of vegetation in shallow water.

non-breeding

★★ **Black-necked Grebe** *Podiceps nigricollis*

| S | S | A | W | COAST, FRESH

Rare breeder; scarce winter visitor to coastal and inland waters mainly in S and W. **ID** Steep forehead and peak of crown above eye. In breeding plumage, has golden tufts on sides of head. In winter, black above and white below. In flight, lacks any white on forewing. Often elusive, disappearing into dense reeds. **NEST** On low mound of waterside vegetation.

non-breeding

★★ Smew *Mergellus albellus* <

| s | s | A | **W** | FRESH

Scarce winter visitor from NE Europe and Siberia to inland waters. **ID** Female and immature drakes small and compact, known as 'red heads'. Adult drake very distinctive, mainly white. In flight, both sexes show similar upperwing pattern. Feeds by diving. Lone birds often rather shy, tending to feed near aquatic vegetation among which they can readily hide.

male

★ Red-breasted Merganser
Mergus serrator

| **S** | **S** | **A** | **W** | COAST, FRESH

Fairly common breeder in freshwater and tidal habitats in N and W, moving to coastal waters in winter. **ID** Smaller and slimmer than Goosander. In female, chestnut of head 'merges' into grey neck. Drake has dark green head and brown breast. In flight, thin black lines divides white inner wing panel. **NEST** Concealed under vegetation or boulder near water.

male

★ Goosander *Mergus merganser*

| **S** | **S** | **A** | **W** | FRESH

Fairly common breeder on rivers and inland waters in N and W, spreading further south in winter. **ID** Large, long, heavy body. Female shows sharp division between chestnut head and grey neck. Drake has dark green head and white underparts. In flight, all-white inner wing panel. **NEST** In hole in tree or bank, or amongst boulders near water.

male

★★ **Scaup** *Aythya marila*

| s | s | A | w | COAST

Fairly common winter visitor, mainly from Iceland, to estuarine and coastal waters. **ID** Marine equivalent of Tufted Duck. In flight, both sexes show broad white wing bar, but drake has black head and neck contrasting with grey back.

female

female

★ **Tufted Duck**
Aythya fuligula

| S | S | A | W | FRESH

Fairly common breeder on lowland waters; common winter visitor from N Europe and Iceland to inland waters. **ID** Commonest diving duck breeding in Britain and Ireland. In flight, both sexes show broad white wing bar; upperparts of drake otherwise all black. **NEST** Under low shrub near water.

★★ **Velvet Scoter**
Melanitta fusca

| s | s | A | w | COAST

Fairly common winter visitor from N Europe to coastal waters, mainly in E. **ID** Longer and bulkier than Common Scoter; white panel often visible on closed wing. In flight, both sexes appear black with white inner wing panel. Dives by slipping under water without a leap. Head held high on wing shaking, when white panel clearly visible.

female

★★ Black Guillemot
Cepphus grille

| S | S | A | W | COAST |

Fairly common resident of rocky areas in Scotland and Ireland. **ID** Smaller than Guillemot, with shorter bill and red legs and feet. In breeding plumage, all black except for large white oval on closed wing. In winter, head and body largely white. In flight, black wings with white ovals at all seasons. Known as Tystie in Scotland. **NEST** In hole in base of cliff or under boulders.

non-breeding

female

★★★ Red-crested Pochard
Netta rufina

| S | S | A | W | FRESH |

Genuine wild birds are rare visitors from S and E Europe; small numbers of feral birds breed mainly in S and E. **ID** One of the largest freshwater diving ducks. Drake's brightly coloured head makes it unmistakable. In flight, both sexes show broad, white wing bar; drake also has white oval on flanks.

★★ Gadwall *Anas strepera*

| S | S | A | W | FRESH |

Scarce breeder mainly in S; fairly common in winter. **ID** White panel often visible on closed wing. Female all brown. In flight, white inner wing panel on female may be very indistinct. Surface feeder, frequently in small groups. **VOICE** Drake gives dry, croaking call, not unlike Mallard. **NEST** On ground in thick vegetation near water.

male

female

male

★★★ Ruddy Shelduck
Tadorna ferruginea

S | **S** | **A** | W FARM, MARSH

Rare visitor from SE Europe and Asia, most (if not all) recent records thought to relate to feral birds. **ID** Goose-like duck with head distinctly paler than body. In flight, upperwing pattern recalls Egyptian Goose.

★ Shelduck
Tadorna tadorna

S | **S** | **A** | **W** COAST, FARM, FRESH, HEATH, MARSH

Common resident around coasts and estuaries, also breeding inland. **ID** One of the most conspicuous and colourful estuarine birds; can appear black and white at a distance. **VOICE** Drake gives characteristic hissing whistle in flight, female a nagging, guttural call. **NEST** Usually in underground burrow.

female

male

★★ Egyptian Goose
Alopochen aegyptiaca

S | **S** | **A** | **W** FARM, FRESH, MARSH, PARK

Scarce introduced resident found mainly in E Anglia. **ID** Strange, pinkish-brown bird. In flight, upperwing pattern recalls Ruddy Shelduck. **VOICE** Loud, husky, wheezing calls given both in flight and on ground. **NEST** In hole in tree.

male

★ **Eider** *Somateria mollissima*

| S | S | A | W | COAST

Common coastal resident in N; smaller numbers also winter in coastal waters of S and E. **ID** Large, short-necked, heavy-looking duck. Eclipse (post-breeding) drake has variable amount of white; female all brown. In flight, heavy looking with broad wings; parties fly in long, straggly lines. **VOICE** Drake gives a loud 'oooo' with an upward inflection at end, as if surprised. **NEST** On ground amongst rocks, fairly close to sea; nest lined with eider down.

★★ **Goldeneye**
Bucephala clangula   < 🦆

| S | S | A | W | COAST, FRESH

Rare localised breeder inland in Scotand; fairly common winter visitor from Scandinavia to both coastal and inland waters. **ID** Large, rounded head with peaked crown. Drake has glossy green head, white breast and flanks. In flight, drake shows more extensive white on upperwing. Dives frequently when feeding. **NEST** In hole in tree, or in nesting box.

female

★ **Wigeon** *Anas penelope*

| S | S | A | W | FRESH, MARSH

Scarce breeder, mainly in N; very common winter visitor from N Europe and Siberia. **ID** Female lacks white wing panel of adult drake. In flight, adult drake shows broad white patch on upperwing. Feeds by grazing, often forming large winter flocks and joining Brent Geese on coastal saltings and marshes. **VOICE** Drake gives characteristic drawn-out whistle. **NEST** On ground in thick waterside vegetation.

male

★ **Great Spotted Woodpecker**
Dendrocopos major

S | **S** | **A** | **W** | FARM, GARDEN, HEATH, PARK, WOOD

Common resident. **ID** Commonest and most widespread of our woodpeckers, a frequent visitor to garden bird feeders. Formerly known as Pied Woodpecker from large, white oval patches on upperparts. **VOICE** Sharp, penetrating 'kee, kee, kee...'. Drums in single rolls. **NEST** In hole in tree.

male

★★ **Lesser Spotted Woodpecker** *Dendrocopos minor*

S | **S** | **A** | **W** | FARM, PARK, WOOD

Fairly common but very localised and declining resident. **ID** Smallest and most sparsely distributed of our woodpeckers. Short, chisel-like bill; lacks red undertail coverts, compared with Great Spotted Woodpecker. Tends to feed high in trees. **VOICE** Similar 'kee' call to Great Spotted Woodpecker but quieter. Drumming carries for a shorter distance than Great Spotted and tends to be in two rolls in rapid succession. **NEST** In hole in tree.

male

★ **Pied Wagtail** *Motacilla alba*

S | **S** | **A** | **W** | BUILDINGS, FARM, GARDEN, MARSH

Very common resident and partial migrant. **ID** Our only small black and white bird with a long tail that is constantly wagged up and down. Adult male has black upperparts; both sexes have blackish rump. **VOICE** Call a disyllabic 'tizzick'. Song a simple twittering incorporating flight call with frequent pauses. **NEST** In hole or cavity in building, wall or other man-made object.

male
breeding

★ **Swallow** *Hirundo rustica*

S | **S** | **A** | **W** | BUILDINGS, FARM, FRESH

Very common summer visitor. **ID** Long, pointed wings and tail streamers. Glossy metallic blue back; red on head visible only at close range; underparts vary from white to chestnut-buff depending on race. Male has longer tail streamers. **VOICE** Rapid twittering at rest and in flight; shrill alarm call. **NEST** Open mud structure on rafters or ledge in cow shed, stable, outhouse, garage or other building.

★ **House Martin** *Delichon urbicum*

| S | S | A | W | BUILDINGS, COAST |

Very common summer visitor. **ID** Short, forked tail with no streamers. Glossy blue-black back and head; white rump and underparts; white feathers cover legs and feet. Glides more than Swallow. **VOICE** A chirruping twitter in flight; shrill alarm call. **NEST** Usually in colony, enclosed mud structure with entrance hole near top, built under eaves or locally on cliffs.

★★ **Dipper** *Cinclus cinclus*

| S | S | A | W | FRESH, MOOR, MOUNTAIN |

Localised resident. **ID** A dumpy, Wren-shaped bird with a short tail, usually seen bobbing on rocks in the middle of fast-flowing streams. May appear black and white at a distance. White eyelid visible as it blinks. Our only passerine that swims. Low, direct flight over water. **VOICE** A sharp, metallic 'zinc'. **NEST** Domed structure with a side entrance, overlooking and often overhanging water.

★★ **Ring Ouzel** *Turdus torquatus*

| S | S | A | W | COAST, MOOR, MOUNTAIN |

Fairly common but localised summer visitor and scarce passage migrant from Scandinavia. **ID** Appears slightly larger and bulkier than Blackbird. A shy bird that is not easily approached, readily flying into cover. **VOICE** Flight call a loud 'tchak, tchak'. Loud song, consisting of repeated double or treble notes with intermittent chuckles. **NEST** On ground in a hollow, or in a rocky crevice, hole in a wall or a stump.

male

★★ **Pied Flycatcher** *Ficedula hypoleuca*

| S | S | A | W | COAST, WOOD |

Localised summer visitor and fairly common autumn passage migrant from Scandinavia. **ID** Both sexes have white wing flashes and white sides to tail. Female and non-breeding birds brown above, paler below. An active bird that is rarely still; when perched, often flicks its tail and one wing. **VOICE** Call a frequently repeated 'whit' or anxious 'phweet'. **NEST** In hole in tree or in a nest box.

male

★ Long-tailed Tit
Aegithalos caudatus

| S | S | A | W | FARM, GARDEN, HEATH, WOOD

Very common resident. **ID** Easily recognised by very small size and extremely long tail. Pink on upperparts. Acrobatic while feeding, usually in pairs or family parties that remain together throughout winter. **VOICE** Constant, noisy trilling calls and thin 'tsee-tsee-tsee'. **NEST** Domed structure built of moss and lichen in thick bush, such as gorse or bramble, or in conifer.

★ Magpie *Pica pica*

| S | S | A | W | FARM, GARDEN, SCRUB

Very common resident. **ID** Noisy, black and white bird with a very long tail, especially evident when flying. At closer range and in sun, glossy metallic sheen on wings of adult. Short, rounded wings in flight with white windows along each primary. Rapid wing beats followed by a brief pause. **VOICE** Well-known alarm call consists of a harsh chattering. **NEST** Domed structure in tree, bush or hedge.

★★ Snow Bunting
Plectrophenax nivalis

| S | S | A | W | COAST, MOUNTAIN

Rare breeder in Scotland; fairly common winter visitor from Greenland, Iceland and Scandinavia. **ID** Male in breeding plumage unmistakable; in winter both sexes have streaked, buff upperparts and white underparts; male has extensive white patches on inner wings. Single birds often very tame, but flocks restless and unapproachable. Feeds in flocks in winter on beaches and coastal fields, resembling drifting snowflakes in flight. **VOICE** Flight call 'prrritt, teu', recalling Little Ringed Plover. Song a brief but musical twitter, often given in flight. **NEST** On ground amongst rocks or boulders.

male breeding

★ Oystercatcher
Haematopus ostralegus

| S | S | A | W | COAST, FARM, FRESH

Common resident, partial migrant and winter visitor, mainly from Iceland and Norway. **ID** One of our most familiar coastal waders, now spreading inland. Distinctive pied plumage and long, stout, orange-red bill. Very noisy both in flight and on ground. **VOICE** Shrill 'peep', repeated many times during piping display in pairs or small groups. **NEST** On beach, dunes, arable and grassy land or amongst rocks.

★★ Avocet
Recurvirostra avosetta

| S | S | A | W | COAST, FRESH, MARSH

Scarce but increasing breeder, wintering largely around estuaries in S and E. **ID** Unmistakable, with upcurved bill and long legs extended in flight. At distance can appear mainly white; if swimming, which it does on occasions, may initially be mistaken for a gull. **VOICE** Loud piping call. **NEST** On open bare mud or shingle, not far from freshwater.

★ Lapwing *Vanellus vanellus*

| S | S | A | W | COAST, FARM, MARSH

Very common but decreasing lowland breeder; abundant winter visitor from N Europe. **ID** One of the characteristic birds of farmland. Appears black and white, but upperparts have greeny-purple iridescence. In flight, black wings contrast with white wing tips and rump. Tumbling display flight in spring. Often in large flocks out of breeding season. Also known as Peewit or Green Plover. **VOICE** Scolding 'peewee'. **NEST** On ground on field or marshland.

★★ **Manx Shearwater** *Puffinus puffinus*

| S | S | A | W | COAST

Very common summer visitor to colonies on offshore islands in
W; elsewhere a fairly common autumn visitor to many coastal
waters. **ID** By far the commonest shearwater; black above and
white below; black cap extends below eye. In flight recalls an auk,
but bursts of stiff-winged flapping interspersed with glides.
VOICE Highly vocal at night in breeding colonies, giving a variety of
raucous crowing sounds. **NEST** In burrow in turf or natural crevice.

bridled
breeding   breeding

★ **Guillemot** *Uria aalge*

| S | S | A | W | COAST

Very common breeder at cliff colonies; fairly common in
most coastal waters in winter. **ID** Penguin-like bird;
upperparts dark brown, but appear black at distance;
slender, pointed bill; short tail held flat on water. In flight,
feet project beyond tail. Some birds have white spectacles in
breeding plumage, known as 'bridled' variety. **NEST** In dense
colonies on open cliff ledges.

★★ **Black Guillemot** *Cepphus grille*

| S | S | A | W | COAST

Fairly common resident of rocky areas in Scotland and Ireland.
ID Smaller than Guillemot, with shorter bill. In winter, our only
auk with an entirely white head. Breeding plumage all black
apart from white oval on wings, red legs and feet. Known as
Tystie in Scotland. **NEST** In hole in base of cliff or under boulder.

non-breeding

breeding

★ **Razorbill** *Alca torda*

| S | S | A | W | COAST

Common breeder at cliff colonies; fairly common in most
coastal waters in winter, but generally less abundant in E than
Guillemot. **ID** Shorter and dumpier than Guillemot; jet black
above and white below; short, deep, stubby bill with vertical
white line; longish, pointed tail often held raised when
swimming. In flight, tail extends beyond feet. **NEST** Concealed
in crevice on cliff or under boulder.

★★ Puffin *Fratercula arctica*

| S | S | A | W | COAST

Fairly common but localised breeder at coastal colonies in N and W; scarce in coastal waters in winter. **ID** The comic of the seabird world with huge, brightly coloured, parrot-like bill in summer; feet orange. In winter has dusky grey cheeks and bill becomes smaller and duller. In flight, dark underwing compared with Guillemot and Razorbill. **NEST** In burrow on grassy slopes by cliffs.

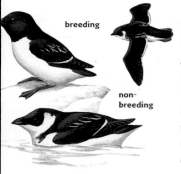

breeding

non-breeding

★★ Little Auk *Alle alle*

| S | S | A | W | COAST

Autumn and winter visitor from the Arctic, in variable numbers to coastal waters. **ID** A scarce visitor, except in 'wreck' years, when large numbers move down from the far N. Very small auk, only half the size of Puffin, with very short stubby bill; often appears neckless. In flight has dark underwing, as does Puffin. Leaps easily from water on taking off and flies with very rapid, whirring wing beats.

★ Great Black-backed Gull
Larus marinus

| S | S | A | W | COAST, FARM

Common coastal resident in N and W, and joined in E by winter visitors from N Europe. **ID** Largest, most maritime of British breeding gulls. More barrel chested than Lesser Black-backed Gull, with very heavy, deep, angular bill; pink legs at all ages. **VOICE** Deeper and gruffer than Herring Gull. **NEST** On top of rock stacks or islands.

breeding

★★ Black Tern *Chlidonias niger*

| S | S | A | W | COAST, FRESH

Scarce or in some years fairly common visitor to both inland and coastal waters, mainly in spring. **ID** Smaller, shorter winged and less rakish than Common Tern. In breeding plumage, has all black head and underparts. Feeds by dipping down to water surface; does not dive.

breeding

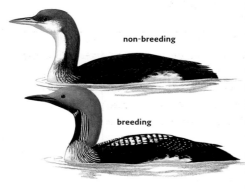

non-breeding

breeding

★★ Black-throated Diver
Gavia arctica

| S | S | A | W | COAST, FRESH

Scarce breeder in Scotland; fairly common winter visitor to selected coastal waters. **ID** Intermediate between Red-throated and Great Northern Divers in size and shape; dagger-like bill held horizontally. In winter, crown dove grey, extending in broad band down side of rear half of neck; white triangle on rear flank. **NEST** Shallow scrape on mound, usually on small island.

non-breeding

breeding

★★ Great Northern Diver
Gavia immer

| S | S | A | W | COAST

Fairly common winter visitor from Iceland and Nearctic to coastal waters, mainly off Scotland and Ireland. **ID** Largest of the three divers; angular head shape with peaked forecrown and thick neck; heavy, dagger-like bill held horizontally. Rather goose-like in flight with slow, deliberate wing beats and large, paddle-like feet extending well beyond tail.

non-breeding

★ Red-throated Diver
Gavia stellata

| S | S | A | W | COAST, FRESH

Fairly common but localised breeder in Scotland; common winter visitor to coastal waters. **ID** Commonest, smallest and slimmest diver; bill uptilted and held pointing skywards. In breeding plumage, deep red velvet throat patch can look black at a distance; vertical black and white stripes on back of neck. Appears long and slim in flight. **NEST** Shallow scrape on mound by shore.

non-breeding

★ Great Crested Grebe
Podiceps cristatus

| S | S | A | W | COAST, FRESH

Widespread resident of lowland waters. **ID** Largest, slimmest and most elegant grebe; long, slender neck and pink bill. Ornate head plumes in breeding plumage. Very long, thin neck in flight with much white on upperwing. **NEST** On mound of aquatic vegetation near water's edge.

★★ Red-necked Grebe
Podiceps grisegena

| S | S | A | W | COAST, FRESH

Scarce winter visitor from NE Europe to coastal waters, mainly in S and E, with a few inland. **ID** Intermediate in size and shape between Slavonian and Great Crested Grebes; in all plumages darker neck than Great Crested Grebe and thickish bill with yellow at base. Rarely seen in full breeding plumage in Britain and Ireland. Leaps up before diving. In flight has shorter neck than Great Crested Grebe with less white on upperwing.

non-breeding

★★ Black-necked Grebe
Podiceps nigricollis

non-breeding

| S | S | A | W | COAST, FRESH

Rare breeder; scarce winter visitor to coastal and inland waters, mainly in S and W. **ID** Steep forehead and peak of crown above red eye; fine, uptilted bill; fluffed-out rear end. In breeding plumage has golden ear tufts on side of head. Often elusive, disappearing into dense reeds. **NEST** On low mound of waterside vegetation.

★★ Slavonian Grebe *Podiceps auritus*

| S | S | A | W | COAST, FRESH

Rare breeder, mainly in Scotland; scarce winter visitor to coastal waters. **ID** Short, straight bill with pale tip, red eye ring and iris at all times of year. In breeding plumage has golden tufts on top of head. The most maritime of our grebes. **NEST** On floating mound of vegetation in shallow water.

non-breeding

★ **Tufted Duck** *Aythya fuligula*

S | S | A | W | FRESH

Fairly common breeder on lowland waters; common winter visitor from N Europe and Iceland to inland waters. **ID** Commonest diving duck breeding in Britain and Ireland; both sexes have yellow eye. Female dull brown with paler flank. In flight, drake has all-black upperparts except for broad white wing bar. **NEST** Under low shrub near water.

male

★★ **Scaup** *Aythya marila*

S | S | A | W | COAST

Fairly common winter visitor, mainly from Iceland, to estuarine and coastal waters. **ID** Marine equivalent of Tufted Duck; rounded head, yellow eye and grey bill. Female dull brown with paler flank. In flight, drake shows pale grey back.

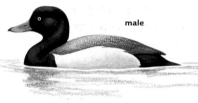

male

★★ **Goldeneye** *Bucephala clangula*

S | S | A | W | COAST, FRESH

Rare localised breeder inland in Scotland; fairly common winter visitor from Scandinavia to both coastal and inland waters. **ID** Large, rounded head with peaked crown; small bill and yellow iris; white panel often visible on closed wing. Female has brown head and greyish body. In flight, drake has broad white patch on inner wing. Dives frequently when feeding. **NEST** In hole in tree, or in nesting box.

male

★★ Long-tailed Duck *Clangula hyemalis*

`S | S | A | W |` COAST

Fairly common winter visitor from Arctic to coastal waters, mainly in N. **ID** Unique amongst wildfowl in having three moults a year, therefore a variety of plumages, with winter adult drake showing the most white. Female generally brown, whitish head and neck with isolated dark cheek patch. In flight, both sexes have all-dark wings.

male non-breeding

★ Goosander *Mergus merganser*

`S | S | A | W |` FRESH

Fairly common breeder on rivers and inland waters in N and W, spreading further south in winter. **ID** Large, long, heavy body; long red bill with hooked tip. At a distance green head of drake appears black. Female has brown head and grey body. **NEST** In hole in tree, bank or amongst boulders near water.

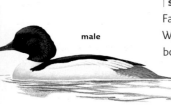

male

★ Shelduck *Tadorna tadorna*

`S | S | A | W |` COAST, FARM, FRESH, HEATH, MARSH

Common resident around coasts and estuaries, also breeding inland. **ID** One of the most conspicuous and colourful estuarine birds; can appear black and white at a distance. Drake larger and more brightly coloured with broader breast band and brighter red knob above bill. **VOICE** Drake gives characteristic hissing whistle in flight, female a nagging guttural call. **NEST** Usually in underground burrow.

female

male

★ Eider *Somateria mollissima*

`S | S | A | W |` COAST

Common coastal resident in N; smaller numbers also winter in coastal waters of S and E. **ID** Large, short-necked, heavy-looking duck; distinctive profile due to long, wedge-shaped bill merging into flat, sloping forehead. Eclipse (post-breeding) drakes show variable amount of white; female all brown. **VOICE** Drake gives a loud 'oooo' with an upward inflection at end, as if surprised. **NEST** On ground amongst rocks, fairly close to sea; nest lined with eider down.

male breeding

★ **Jackdaw** *Corvus monedula*

| S | S | A | W | BUILDINGS, COAST, FARM, GARDEN, PARK, WOOD

Very common resident. **ID** Noticeably smaller and dumpier than Rook or Carrion Crow. All dark, although grey nape and cheek; white iris visible at close range. A jaunty, gregarious bird, forms a life-long bond and is usually seen in pairs. **VOICE** Call an almost musical 'jack'. **NEST** In hole or cavity in tree, building, chimney or cave, in a loose colony.

★★ **Chough** *Pyrrhocorax pyrrhocorax*

| S | S | A | W | COAST, FARM

Fairly common but very localised resident. **ID** Size of Jackdaw. The only all-black bird with a long, red, decurved bill. Highly sociable and rarely seen alone. Performs acrobatic aerial manoeuvres. **VOICE** Jackdaw-like call but higher pitched 'cheow', from which it gets its name. **NEST** On ledge in cave.

★ **Carrion Crow** *Corvus corone*

| S | S | A | W | FARM, HEATH, MOOR, PARK, WOOD

Abundant resident. **ID** All-black plumage; flatter crown than Rook and stouter bill with down-curved upper mandible. In flight, broader wings and shorter tail than Rook. Does occur in groups, but more often seen singly or in pairs. **VOICE** Usually gives a trisyllabic 'cor, cor, cor'. **NEST** Generally in a fairly tall tree.

★ **Rook** *Corvus frugilegus*

| S | S | A | W | FARM, PARK, WOOD

Abundant resident. **ID** All-black plumage; peaked crown rising steeply from base of long, narrow, pointed bill; area of bare, whitish skin around base of bill; triangular swelling rising from lower mandible in breeding season only. In flight, appears to have narrower, longer wings and a longer, more diamond-shaped tail than Carrion Crow. Gregarious and often found in mixed flocks with Jackdaws. **VOICE** Most vocal at rookery, a loud 'car, car', less harsh than crow. **NEST** In tree-top colonies.

★★ **Raven** *Corvus corax* >

| S | S | A | W | COAST, FARM, MOOR, MOUNTAIN, WOOD

Fairly common but localised resident. **ID** Our largest crow, even bigger than a Buzzard. All-black plumage; very heavy bill; shaggy throat feathers. In flight, long wings and a long, wedge-shaped tail. Pairs for life and often seen with partner. **VOICE** A deep, croaking 'crark', recalling a distant dog barking. **NEST** On rock ledge or in fork of tree.

★★ **Black Grouse** *Tetrao tetrix* >

| S | S | A | W | FARM, HEATH, MOOR, WOOD

Localised and declining resident. **ID** Female brown, barred darker, some with a notched tail. Males gather into communal display groups, called 'leks', in spring. Male also known as Blackcock and female as Greyhen. **VOICE** Male gives bubbling calls, audible at long range. **NEST** On ground amongst low plants.

male

★★ **Capercaillie** *Tetrao urogallus* >

| S | S | A | W | WOOD

Fairly common but localised and declining resident in Scotland. **ID** Largest grouse in the world, inhabiting Scots pine forests. Male 30 per cent larger than female, which is brown and barred darker, with a rounded tail. Males gather into 'leks' (display groups) in evening. **VOICE** Dawn song a series of accelerating clicking calls, followed by a 'pop' and a terminal hiss. Male display involves a mixture of guttural, belching-like calls. **NEST** On ground amongst undergrowth, often at base of pine tree.

male

★ **Swift** *Apus apus*

S | S | A | W | BUILDINGS, FRESH

Common summer visitor and passage migrant from Europe.
ID The all-dark, Swallow-like bird that flies around houses
screaming on summer evenings. Larger than Swallow, with
long, sickle-shaped wings and shallowly forked tail. Exclusively
aerial except when nesting. Highly sociable and pairs for life.
VOICE Shrill, screaming calls, often while flying in tightly knit
flocks. **NEST** In roof space of building, entering under eaves or
through broken tiles, occasionally in cavities in rocky cliffs.

★★ **Black Redstart** *Phoenicurus ochruros*

S | S | A | W | BUILDINGS, COAST

male

Rare breeder; scarce winter visitor and passage migrant from
Europe. **ID** Often very elusive. Constantly quivering bright
chestnut tail. Only adult male is black; female brownish-grey.
Usually seen perched on building or fence, from where it drops
to feed briefly on ground. **VOICE** Scolding 'tucc-tucc' and
snappy 'fist'. Short, loud, warbling song with terminal flourish.
NEST In recess or hole in building or at derelict industrial areas.

★ **Blackbird** *Turdus merula*

S | S | A | W | FARM, GARDEN, PARK, WOOD

Abundant resident; common winter visitor and
passage migrant, mainly in autumn from
N Europe. **ID** One of our most familiar birds.
Male all black with a yellow bill and orbital ring;
female dark brown with streaks on breast.
VOICE Clucks when alarmed and gives a
distinctive chattering call in flight. Song a
fairly short, loud, melodious warbling, the whole
song being repeated at frequent intervals.
NEST In low tree, shrub or hedgerow.

male

★★ **Ring Ouzel** *Turdus torquatus*

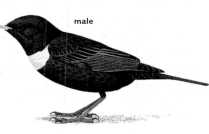

| S | S | A | W | COAST, MOOR, MOUNTAIN

Fairly common but localised summer visitor; scarce passage migrant from Scandinavia. **ID** Appears slightly larger and bulkier than Blackbird. Female brownish-black with off-white crescent across breast and variable pale scaling on body. A shy bird that is not easily approached, readily flying into cover. **VOICE** Flight call a loud 'tchak, tchak'. Loud song consisting of repeated double or treble notes with intermittent chuckles. **NEST** On ground in a hollow, or in a rocky crevice, hole in a wall or a stump.

male

male

★ **Starling** *Sturnus vulgaris*

| S | S | A | W | BUILDINGS, FARM, GARDEN, PARK, WOOD

Abundant but declining resident and winter visitor from Europe. **ID** A gregarious and quarrelsome visitor to many gardens. In summer, appears all black with yellow bill, the base of the bill being blue in male and pink in female, which also has a white iris. Walks rather than hops. **VOICE** Rapid, noisy chattering incorporating the calls of many other local species, e.g. Magpie, House Sparrow, Curlew, etc. **NEST** In hole in tree, wall of building, roof or nest box.

★★ **Spotted Redshank**
Tringa erythropus

<

| S | S | A | W | FRESH, MARSH

Scarce passage migrant and winter visitor from Fennoscandia. **ID** Elegant, slim wader with long, fine bill and long legs; very pale grey plumage in winter. Will wade in deeper water, where it feeds by swimming and upending. **VOICE** Flight call a disyllabic 'chewit'.

breeding

★ **Hooded Crow** *Corvus cornix*

| S | S | A | W | FARM, MOOR, PARK, WOOD

Very common resident in Scotland and Ireland; elsewhere scarce winter visitor from Scandinavia. **ID** Otherwise known as Grey Crow. Wide zone of hybridisation between the breeding ranges of Carrion and Hooded Crows. **VOICE** Hoarse croaking as for Carrion Crow. **NEST** In tall tree, on cliff ledge or rocky outcrop.

★ **Magpie** *Pica pica*

| S | S | A | W | FARM, GARDEN, SCRUB

Very common resident. **ID** Noisy, black and white bird with a very long tail, especially evident when flying. At closer range and in sun, glossy metallic sheen on wings of adult. Short, rounded wings in flight with white windows along each primary. Rapid wing beats followed by a brief pause. **VOICE** Well-known alarm call is a harsh chattering. **NEST** Domed structure in tree, bush or hedge.

★★★ **Rose-coloured Starling** *Sturnus roseus*

| S | S | A | W | FARM, GARDEN

Rare visitor from E Europe and Asia. **ID** Size and behaviour as Starling, with which it usually associates, but adult unmistakable. **VOICE** As Starling.

male breeding

★ **Reed Bunting** *Emberiza schoeniclus*

| S | S | A | W | FARM, FRESH, REEDS, SCRUB

Very common resident and partial migrant. **ID** One of the most familiar birds of reedbeds and reed-fringed pools due to the male's habit of singing from a prominent perch, such as the top of a reed stem or a bush. Heavily streaked with white sides to tail and a small dark bill. In breeding plumage, only male has extensive black head and throat. **VOICE** Call a distinct 'sieoo' with a downward inflection. Song, which starts slowly but speeds up, a short, discordant collection of notes: 'tseek, tseek, tseek, tississik'. **NEST** On ground in grassy tussock or clump of rushes, or in a low bush.

★★ Lapland Bunting
Calcarius lapponicus

| S | S | A | W | COAST, FARM |

Scarce winter visitor and passage migrant from
Fennoscandia. **ID** Stockier than Reed Bunting and
male has more extensive black and darker upperparts
in breeding plumage. Female could be mistaken for
female Reed Bunting. Usually very wary, running
along ground to escape detection rather than taking
flight. **VOICE** Flight call a short rattle followed by a
plaintive note: 'ticky, tick, tioo'. Can sound very similar
to Snow Bunting.

male breeding

male
breeding

★★ Brambling *Fringilla montifringilla*

| S | S | A | W | FARM, GARDEN, WOOD |

Occasional breeder in Scotland; common winter visitor,
mainly from Fennoscandia. **ID** Size and shape of
Chaffinch; orange tinge to the breast in all plumages,
with dark, round spots on flanks; rump white.
Associates with Chaffinches; often found feeding on
beech mast in winter. **VOICE** Loud, harsh, questioning
'tchweep' and quiet 'tchup'.

★ Stonechat *Saxicola torquatc*

| S | S | A | W | HEATH, MOOR, SCRUB |

Common but declining resident and partial migrant.
ID Plumper and more upright than Whinchat.
Male much brighter than female, with black head
and white half collar in breeding plumage.
Often seen on top of bushes and fence posts,
when it characteristically jerks wings and tail.
VOICE Scolding 'wheest, tchack, tchack' like two
stones being knocked together. Song rather quiet,
short and scratchy, recalling Dunnock. **NEST** On or
near ground in vegetation at base of bush.

male

★ **Blackcap** *Sylvia atricapilla*

| S | S | A | W | FARM, GARDEN, WOOD

Very common summer visitor; scarce winter visitor from Central Europe. **ID** Male grey with black cap. Female browner with brown cap. Both sexes lack any white in the tail. Blackcaps breeding in Britain and Ireland winter around W Mediterranean. **VOICE** Call a hard 'tac, tac', louder than Lesser Whitethroat. Song a rich, fluty warble, more varied but less sustained than Garden Warbler. **NEST** Above ground in low bush, brambles, evergreen or other woody vegetation.

male

★ **Marsh Tit** *Poecile palustris*

| S | S | A | W | GARDEN, PARK, WOOD

Common but declining resident. **ID** Very similar to Willow Tit and often best separated by voice, but Marsh Tit has glossy black cap, small, neat, black bib and paler underparts, lacks pale panel on closed wing; viewed from below tail appears square ended. Often found in pairs, even in winter. **VOICE** Call an explosive 'pitchoo' and nasal 'tchair'. Song a fairly loud and repetitive 'tchupp, tchupp, tchupp...'. **NEST** In hole in tree or stump.

★★ **Willow Tit** *Poecile montana*

| S | S | A | W | WOOD

Fairly common but declining resident. **ID** Very similar to Marsh Tit and best to confirm identification by voice. Has dull black cap, more extensive bib that is wider at lower border, buffer flanks and pale edges to secondaries on closed wing; viewed from below tail appears more rounded. Despite names, Willow Tits tend to be found in damper areas of woodland than Marsh Tits. **VOICE** Call easily recognised once learnt: 'tzi, tzi, chaar, chaar, chaar', the last three notes rather drawn out and hoarse. Song 'tu, tu, tu, t...', recalling Nightingale or Wood Warbler. **NEST** Excavates its own nesting cavity in rotten tree stump.

female

male

★ **Bullfinch** *Pyrrhula pyrrhula*

| S | S | A | W | FARM, GARDEN, SCRUB, WOOD

Very common resident. **ID** Retiring habits, presence often betrayed by the flash of a white rump as it flies away. Plump, rounded breast and bull neck. Male bright reddish-pink on underparts. **VOICE** Haunting, piping 'hoee' contact call. Weak, creaky song rarely heard. **NEST** In bush or shrub.

★ **Coal Tit** *Periparus ater*

<

| S | S | A | W | GARDEN, WOOD

Very common resident. **ID** A typical bird of coniferous woodland, its thin bill allowing it to feed between pine needles. White patch on nape; broad black bib. **VOICE** Call 'tsui' with rising inflection at end and other thin calls very like those of Goldcrest. Song an oft-repeated 'peechoo'. **NEST** In hole, low down, on ground, in bank, in rock crevice or amongst tree roots.

★ **Great Tit** *Parus major*

| S | S | A | W | FARM, GARDEN, PARK, WOOD

Abundant resident. **ID** Largest of our tits. Black and white head pattern; black vertical band along centre of yellow underparts, narrower and duller on female. **VOICE** Calls rich and varied, no two individuals sounding exactly alike. Contact notes very similar to Chaffinch's 'spink' or Marsh Tit's 'tchair, tchair'. Commonest song is a variation on 'teacher, teacher, teacher', recalling the sound of a bicycle tyre being pumped up. **NEST** In hole in tree, brickwork or other man-made object, or a nest box.

★★ **Storm Petrel** *Hydrobates pelagicus*

`S` | `S` | `A` | `W` | COAST

Very common summer visitor to colonies on offshore islands in N and W; elsewhere scarce autumn visitor to coastal waters. **ID** Smallest and darkest petrel in Britain and Ireland; all dark except for white rump and white bar on underwing, but neither always easy to see. In flight recalls House Martin but fluttering and bat-like. **VOICE** Gives a purring call with a terminal hiccup from within nesting burrows. **NEST** In tunnel burrowed in soft soil or cavity in rocks or stones, such as old wall.

★★ **Leach's Petrel** *Oceanodroma leucorhoa*

`S` | `S` | `A` | `W` | COAST

Common summer visitor to colonies on a few offshore islands in N and W; elsewhere scarce autumn visitor to coastal waters. **ID** Larger than Storm Petrel; all dark except for paler wing panel and white rump, but this is less obvious than in Storm Petrel. Stronger flight than Storm Petrel. **VOICE** A series of purring calls, more varied than Storm Petrel, from within nesting burrows. **NEST** In tunnel in soil or cavity under stones or rocks.

★ **Arctic Skua** *Stercorarius parasiticus*

`S` | `S` | `A` | `W` | COAST, MOOR

Common summer visitor to coastal and island colonies in Scotland, and elsewhere to coastal waters, mainly in autumn. **ID** Gull-like seabird with more pointed wings and dashing, falcon-like flight. Occurs in pale, intermediate and dark colour form. Dark form may appear black at distance and in poor light. In flight, narrower wings with less distinct white flashes than Pomarine Skua; also has elongated central tail feathers in fresh breeding plumage. Chases other seabirds until victim disgorges food, which is then caught in mid-air (known as 'kleptoparasitism'). **NEST** Shallow depression in grass, heather or moss.

dark form

dark form

★★ **Pomarine Skua**
Stercorarius pomarinus

| S | s | A | W | COAST

Scarce visitor from Arctic, mainly in autumn to coastal
waters in S and W. **ID** Between Arctic and Great Skuas
in size; heavy chested. Dark form may appear black at
distance and in poor light. Pale form has more
complete dark breast band than Arctic Skua. In flight,
broader wings with very distinct white flashes and
often a double crescent on underwing, spoon-shaped
central tail projections in fresh breeding plumage;
slower flight than Arctic Skua. Feeds by
kleptoparasitism (see above).

★★ **Great Skua** *Stercorarius skua*

| S | S | A | w | COAST, MOOR

Fairly common summer visitor to coastal and island
colonies in Scotland, and elsewhere to coastal waters,
mainly in autumn. **ID** Largest and heaviest skua, the
size of Herring Gull; dark brown with distinct white
patches on upper and underwings; minimal central
tail projections. In poor light or at a distance may
appear black. Kills and eats birds as small as petrels
and as large as swans, as well as chasing seabirds, up
to size of Gannet, for disgorged food. Also known as
Bonxie. **NEST** Depression in grass, heather or moss.

breeding

★★ **Black Guillemot** *Cepphus grille*

| S | S | A | W | COAST

Fairly common resident of rocky coasts in Scotland and
Ireland. **ID** Smaller than Guillemot, with shorter bill. In
breeding plumage, all black except for large white oval on
closed wing. In winter, head and body largely white. In flight,
black wings with white ovals at all seasons. Known as Tystie
in Scotland. **NEST** In hole in base of cliff or under boulder.

★ Cormorant *Phalacrocorax carbo*

| S | S | A | W | COAST, FRESH

Common resident around many rocky coasts and at
some inland sites; more widespread inland in winter.
ID Large, heavy looking and long necked; peak of
crown at rear of head; strong, hooked bill with area of
bare, yellowish skin at base. Swims low in water,
when long tail may be visible (compare with divers)
and bill held pointing slightly upwards. Often sits
on groynes or posts with wings outstretched.
NEST On cliffs or inland in trees.

breeding

breeding

★ Shag *Phalacrocorax aristotelis*

| S | S | A | W | COAST

Common resident around many rocky coasts, scarce
inland. **ID** Smaller and slimmer than Cormorant;
smaller, more rounded head, with peak of crown
above eye and pencil-thin bill. In flight, has shorter,
straighter neck than Cormorant and flies more
rapidly, low down over the surface of the water
without any glides. Leaps out of water before diving.
NEST On cliffs or rocky ledge.

★ Common Scoter
Melanitta nigra

| S | S | A | W | COAST

Rare localised breeder in Scotland and Ireland;
common winter visitor from Iceland and Scandinavia
to coastal waters. **ID** The commonest sea duck off
the coasts of England, Wales and Ireland. Both sexes
mainly dark, but female has paler cheek. Rests in
dense rafts on the sea, often diving to feed in unison,
with small leap before submerging. Dips head on
wing shaking. **NEST** On ground near freshwater
lake or pool.

male

★★ Velvet Scoter
Melanitta fusca

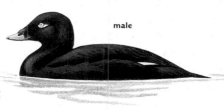

| s | s | **A** | **w** | COAST |

Fairly common winter visitor from N Europe to coastal waters, mainly in E. **ID** Longer and bulkier than Common Scoter; large, wedge-shaped bill; white panel often visible on closed wing. Female dark brown, often with pale cheek patch. Dives by slipping under water without a leap. Head held high on wing shaking, when white panel is clearly visible.

male

★ Moorhen
Gallinula chloropus

| **s** | **s** | **A** | **w** | FARM, FRESH, MARSH |

Very common lowland resident. **ID** The familiar black water bird of village ponds. All dark except for fragmented white line along flanks and white under tail. Moves head back and forth while swimming; flicks tail while walking. **VOICE** Explosive bubbling call and metallic 'kek, kek'. **NEST** Bulky platform of dead vegetation on or by water.

★ Coot *Fulica atra*

| **s** | **s** | **A** | **w** | FRESH, MARSH |

Common lowland resident; winter visitor from NW Europe. **ID** White frontal shield. In flight, paler grey flight feathers are clearly visible. Generally found on larger, more open areas of water, often in large, loose flocks. Swims with gently nodding head; frequent dives preceded by a small leap before bobbing back to surface. Paddles along surface of water before taking off. Argumentative and strongly territorial. **VOICE** Loud, explosive, repetitive 'kruck'. **NEST** Bulky pile of dead reeds on or by water.

★★ **Pomarine Skua** *Stercorarius pomarinus*

S | S | **A** | **W** | COAST

Scarce visitor from Arctic, mainly in autumn to coastal waters in S and W. **ID** Between Arctic and Great Skuas in size; heavy chested. Pale form has more complete dark breast band, more extensive yellow on face and heavier bill with pink base compared with Arctic Skua; also spoon-shaped central tail projections in fresh breeding plumage. Dark form brown. In flight, broader wings with very distinct white flashes and often a double crescent on underwing, and slower flight than Arctic Skua. Chases other seabirds until victim disgorges food, which is then caught in mid-air (known as 'kleptoparasitism').

pale form

★ **Arctic Skua** *Stercorarius parasiticus*

S | **S** | **A** | W | COAST, MOOR

Common summer visitor to coastal and island colonies in Scotland, and elsewhere to coastal waters, mainly in autumn. **ID** Gull-like seabird with more pointed wings and dashing, falcon-like flight. Occurs in pale, intermediate and dark colour morphs. Dark form brown. In flight, narrower wings with less distinct white flashes compared with Pomarine Skua; also has elongated pointed central tail feathers in fresh breeding plumage. Feeds by kleptoparasitism (see above). **NEST** Shallow depression in grass, heather or moss.

pale form

★★★ **Long-tailed Skua** *Stercorarius longicaudus*

S | S | **A** | W | COAST

Generally a rare autumn visitor from Arctic and N Europe to coastal waters, mainly in S and E England, and spring passage migrant past Outer Hebrides. **ID** Rarest and smallest of the four skuas, with long, slim wings recalling tern; short, slender bill, basal half blue-grey. In flight, has grey-brown upperwing coverts contrasting with black flight feathers and minimal white flash; also very long central tail feathers in fresh breeding plumage. Feeds from surface of sea, as well as by kleptoparasitism (see above).

pale form

★ Black-headed Gull
Chroicocephalus ridibundus

S | S | A | W | COAST, FARM, FRESH

Very common breeder around inland and coastal waters; abundant winter visitor from N Europe to most areas except the uplands. **ID** The commonest and most familiar inland gull, also the smallest of the common gulls. Black spot behind eye replaces dark hood in winter. Immature has brown bars across upperwings and black tip to tail. The only common gull to have a white leading edge on the outer wing. **NEST** On open ground, often in large colonies.

breeding

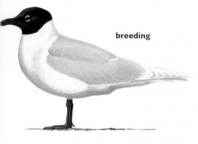

breeding

★★ Mediterranean Gull
Larus melanocephalus

S | S | A | W | COAST

Rare localised breeder, usually in Black-headed Gull colonies; elsewhere scarce winter visitor from Central Europe, but becoming more numerous. **ID** Slightly larger than Black-headed Gull with stouter bill and longer legs. Black smudge behind eye in winter at all ages. In flight, adult appears white-winged. **VOICE** Distinctive, almost cat-like 'mee-ow'. **NEST** On ground in gull colony.

★★ Little Gull *Hydrocoloeus minutus*

S | S | A | W | COAST

Scarce winter visitor and passage migrant from NE Europe to coastal waters, occasionally inland. **ID** Our smallest and daintiest gull. Black spot behind eye and darkish cap replace hood in winter. In flight wing tips appear rounded and adult is white-winged above, but has distinctly dark underwing. Feeds by dipping tern-like to snatch food from surface of water.

breeding

★ **Arctic Tern** *Sterna paradisaea*

`S S A W` COAST

Common summer visitor to coastal colonies, mainly in Scotland and Ireland. **ID** Slightly smaller and daintier than Common Tern, with shorter neck and bill and longer tail streamers; bill entirely blood red in breeding plumage; very short legs. In **breeding** flight, underwing has neat black line along trailing edge of outer feathers on otherwise pure white primaries. Sometimes takes food from surface of water like Black Tern. **VOICE** A drawn-out 'prree-ah'. **NEST** In colony on sand, shingle or grass near the coast.

★ **Common Tern** *Sterna hirundo*

`S S A W` COAST, FRESH

Common and widely dispersed summer visitor to colonies bordering coast and on inland waters. **ID** Pure white underparts; black-tipped red bill is longer than in Arctic Tern. In flight, dark wedge on outer upperwing and fairly broad, ill-defined, dark trailing edge to primaries on underwing. Hovers and dives for food. **VOICE** Noisy and quarrelsome, a series of 'kierri-kierri-kierri'. **NEST** On ground in colony on sand or shingle bank, or on islands on freshwater lakes.

breeding

★★★ **Roseate Tern** *Sterna dougallii*

`S S A W` COAST

Rare summer visitor to a small number of well-scattered colonies. **ID** The most elegant and beautiful of the breeding terns. Size of Common Tern but with paler upperwing recalling small Sandwich Tern, a longer, darker bill and very long tail streamers. In breeding plumage has pink flush on breast and **breeding** dark red base to bill. In flight, wings white apart from a narrow black wedge along leading edge of primaries. Dives powerfully into water to feed. **VOICE** Distinctly disyllabic 'tchivik', likened to flight call of Spotted Redshank. **NEST** On ground in coastal colony, often amongst other species of terns.

⋆ **Sandwich Tern**
Sterna sandvicensis

| S | S | A | W | COAST |

Common but localised summer visitor to scattered coastal colonies. **ID** Large tern with a long, thin, black bill with a yellow tip, shaggy crest and short tail. In flight, appears whiter than other terns. Feeds by flying along with bill pointing down, before closing wings and diving rapidly into water like a miniature Gannet. **VOICE** Distinctive grating 'kerrick'. **NEST** On sand or shingle banks in large colonies.

breeding

⋆⋆ **Little Tern** *Sternula albifrons*

| S | S | A | W | COAST |

Fairly common summer visitor to coastal colonies. **ID** Very small, noisy tern with rapid wing beats. Hovers just above water surface before diving to catch fish. **VOICE** Oft-repeated, rasping, chattering calls. **NEST** In colonies on sandy or shingle beaches.

breeding

⋆⋆ **Black Tern** *Chlidonias niger*

| S | S | A | W | COAST, FRESH |

Scarce or in some years fairly common visitor to both inland and coastal waters, mainly in spring. **ID** Smaller, shorter winged and less rakish than Common Tern. In breeding plumage has all black head and underparts. Feeds by dipping down to water surface; does not dive.

non-breeding

Societies and Journals

With over a million members, the Royal Society for the Protection of Birds (RSPB) is one of the largest conservation organisations in the world. As well as conferring entry to its many reserves around Britain and Ireland, membership also brings the quarterly magazine *Birds*, ideal for those taking up birdwatching for the first time.

Most counties have their own Wildlife Trusts, most of which own or look after local reserves. The field and evening meetings that the county trusts organise enable beginners to meet other people with a similar interest in birds and other aspects of our wildlife.

For those birdwatchers interested in helping with survey work, such as the *Garden Bird Feeding Survey* or the *Bird Atlas 2007–11*, the British Trust for Ornithology (BTO) is the organisation to join. Members also receive the bimonthly magazine *BTO News*. Similar organisations in Scotland and Ireland are the Scottish Ornithologists' Club and BirdWatch Ireland respectively.

Further Reading

In addition to the popular magazines of the RSPB and BTO just mentioned, *Birdwatch* and *Bird Watching* are published monthly and include some excellent articles aimed at beginners, as well as tips on birdwatching techniques and reviews of equipment. While many newcomers will be content to identify the common birds, others will hopefully move on to the less frequently encountered species not illustrated in this book.

Without doubt, the most comprehensive and best illustrated field guide to the birds of Britain and Europe is *Collins Bird Guide* by Killian Mullarney, Lars Svensson, Dan Zetterström and Peter Grant. Another very valuable book illustrating and describing the finer points of identification of the more confusing British birds is *The Macmillan Field Guide to Bird Identification* by Alan Harris, Laurel Tucker and Keith Vinicombe.

Some Useful Addresses

Birdwatch, Solo Publishing Ltd, The Chocolate Factory, 5 Clarendon Road, London N22 6XJ, www.birdwatch.co.uk

Bird Watching, Media House, Lynchwood, Peterborough PE2 6EA, www.greatmagazines.co.uk (and search for 'Bird Watching')

BirdWatch Ireland, Midlands Office, Crank House, Banagher, Co. Offaly, Ireland, www.birdwatchireland.ie

British Trust for Ornithology, The Nunnery, Thetford, Norfolk IP24 2PU, www.bto.org

Royal Society for the Protection of Birds, The Lodge, Sandy, Bedfordshire SG19 2DL, www.rspb.org.uk

Scottish Ornithologists' Club, Waterston House, Aberlady, East Lothian EH32 0PY, www.the-soc.org.uk

Glossary

Adult A bird in its final adult plumage.

Axilla The armpit.

Breeder A species that breeds annually in Britain and/or Ireland.

Breeding plumage That acquired by birds (usually males) during the breeding season, often brightly coloured.

Breeding season The time of year during which birds pair up, nest and raise their young.

Call Often single notes given by birds to maintain contact with their family and/or other flock members, or to act as warning signals to other birds nearby when danger threatens.

Carpal joint The bend in the wing.

Colony A gathering of birds of the same species nesting in the same area.

Colour morph A different-coloured variety of a species.

Contact call A call given by a bird to maintain contact with members of its family or other flock members.

Coverts Feathers that overlie the bases of the flight feathers and tail.

Crepuscular Active at dawn and dusk.

Dabbling duck One that feeds on the surface of the water and does not generally dive.

Decurved bill One that is curved downwards.

Disyllabic A call in two parts.

Diurnal Active by day.

Diving duck One that habitually feeds by diving and swimming underwater.

Eclipse plumage The brown, female-like plumage into which male ducks moult after the breeding season; during this period they are flightless, in order to aid concealment.

Escapes Free-flying birds that have escaped from captivity.

Eyebrow A usually pale stripe above the eye, also known as the supercilium.

Eye stripe A usually dark stripe through the eye.

Fennoscandia Finland and Scandinavia.

Feral species One that has a self-sustaining population in Britain and/or Ireland, but that originally escaped from captivity and did not arrive naturally.

First-winter A bird in its first winter; usually referring to the first plumage that appears after the juvenile plumage.

Fledgling A young bird that has just left the nest and in passerines is capable of flight.

Flight call A call given by a bird in flight to maintain contact with others of the same species.

Fresh breeding plumage The plumage of breeding birds at the start of the breeding season before it has become worn.

Grazing Generally used to refer to waterfowl that feed on short grass.

Host The species always chosen by an individual Cuckoo to raise its young, by laying eggs in the nest of that species.

Immature A bird in any but adult plumage, generally not old enough to be sexually active.

Introduced species One that does not occur naturally in Britain and/or Ireland but has been introduced at some time in the past by humans.

Juvenile Generally used to refer to a bird still in its first plumage, grown before fledging.

Mandible The upper and lower sections of the bill.

Moult The replacement of feathers, often on an annual basis.

Moustachial stripe A narrow stripe, often dark, running from the base of the bill and along the lower edge of the cheek.

Nearctic The Arctic and temperate parts of N America.

Nocturnal Active by night.

Nominate race The first race of a species to have been named.

Orbital ring A circle of bare, unfeathered skin around the eye, usually white or pale in colour.

Partial migrant Used of a species in which only part of the population migrates away from the breeding area.

Passage migrant Used of a species that passes through Britain and/or Ireland but generally does not remain for any length of time.

Passerine A member of the order Passeriformes, commonly known as perching birds.

Polygamous Mating with more than one partner.

Polygynous Of a male, mating with more than one partner.

Primaries The outermost flight feathers, generally ten in number.

Race Another name for a subspecies.

Raptor A diurnal bird of prey.

Resident A species that spends the entire year in Britain and/or Ireland, often in the same general area.

Secondaries The innermost flight feathers between the primaries and the bird's body.

Song Most passerines have a song that is used by the male to attract a mate and to define its territory.

Song flight A flight undertaken by a singing bird.

Speculum A patch of often highly coloured and iridescent feathers on the secondaries of ducks.

Summer visitor Used of a species that spends the summer months in Britain and/or Ireland, usually arriving in the spring and departing in the autumn.

Upending A method of feeding used by waterfowl during which they place their head and neck under water at the same time as swinging up their tail end.

Vagrants Very rare, non-breeding visitors to Britain and/or Ireland.

Vermiculated Covered with a pattern of fine wavy lines.

Wader A commonly used term for most members of the order Charadriiformes, many of which inhabit the water's edge.

Winter visitor Used of a species that spends the winter months in Britain and/or Ireland, usually arriving in the autumn and departing in the spring.

Index